"Richard D. Phillips' *Jesus the Evangelist* is exactly what a paranoid and paralyzed church needs to hear in order to do the essential work of witnessing for Jesus Christ! In a day when so-called 'practical' books are synonymous with fluffy books, here's a solid, readable work for the 'average Christian.' Phillips' study of John 1, 3, and 4 takes us beyond clever techniques to biblical faithfulness, and beyond entertaining communication to sound theology in evangelism. He does a masterful job of helping us learn from God's Word principles for evangelism, the theology of the gospel, and Jesus' own practice in evangelism. Consequently, the reader is moved beyond apathy to action, to proclaiming the good news that Jesus the Son of God has come into the world to take away the sins of all those who repent and believe on Him. Readers of this volume will learn how to evangelize the real people around them from the only real Savior, Jesus Christ. Every pastor should buy two boxes of *Jesus the Evangelist* and give them away to members."

—REV. THABITI ANYABWILE, SENIOR PASTOR
First Baptist Church of Grand Cayman

"Richard Phillips has written a very helpful book that every serious Christian should read. Evangelism is not an afterthought in the Christian life. It is how God has ordained to glorify Himself in the salvation of sinners. Rev. Phillips explains this by showing how Jesus is both the evangel and the Great Evangelist. In the process, he challenges both apathy and superficiality in the great work of making disciples. I highly recommend this book!"

—DR. THOMAS K. ASCOL, SENIOR PASTOR
Grace Baptist Church, Cape Coral, Fla.
and Executive Director, Founders Ministries

Jesus *the* EVANGELIST

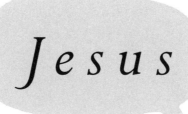

Jesus

the EVANGELIST

Learning to share
the gospel from the
book *of* John

RICHARD D. PHILLIPS

Reformation Trust

P U B L I S H I N G

A DIVISION OF LIGONIER MINISTRIES · ORLANDO, FLORIDA

Library of Congress Cataloging-in-Publication Data
    Phillips, Richard D. (Richard Davis), 1960-
  Jesus the evangelist : learning to share the gospel from the book of John /
  Richard D. Phillips.
      p. cm.
  Includes indexes.
  ISBN 1-56769-088-2
  1. Bible. N.T. John I-IV–Criticism, interpretation, etc. 2. Witness bearing
(Christianity) 3. Evangelistic work. I. Title.
  BS2615.6.W54P45 2007
  226.5'06–dc22

                           2007015925

To

Mrs. Toni Barnhill

Proverbs 31:25

TABLE OF CONTENTS

PREFACE

This book arose from my study of the Gospel of John for a series of expository sermons. Right from the start, I was interested in John's strong emphasis on the theme of gospel witness, and my sermons frequently stressed the privilege and obligation of evangelism. I was also struck by the fact that so much of the material unique to the book of John involves Jesus' personal evangelism. It occurred to me that the material on evangelism in the fourth Gospel is so strong and informative that a book putting some of it together would be a real benefit to the church. The result is *Jesus the Evangelist*, which I hope will both motivate and instruct the practice of evangelism among Christians.

I have two main audiences in mind. The first is composed of the many committed and biblically motivated Christians who do little in the way of evangelism. One often hears that Christians interested in theology show little zeal for sharing the gospel. While I believe this to be completely illogical, I have found in practice that there is something to the charge. This book, then, is intended to enhance the zeal of such believers by showing John's clear mandate for evangelism and to embolden their witness with biblical instruction and encouragement.

My other audience is made up of zealous witnesses who would profit from strong biblical reflection on Jesus' own approach to evangelism. Much of what passes for evangelism today is nothing of the sort. The sad result is that many purported converts have not truly come to faith in Jesus. One is saved by believing the gospel, and to believe the gospel one must hear it. This means that Christian witnesses must know and communicate the gospel and its biblical content. In my view, our generation could profit from a strong dose of biblical reform, so that converts are not merely added to the rolls of our churches but actually receive eternal life through a living faith in the Jesus of the Bible.

If either of these goals is advanced by this book, I will be greatly recompensed for my labor in writing it. May God bless these studies of His Word to motivate His people in their witnessing and to inform their witness so that the gospel is heard with clarity, truth, and conviction.

This book is dedicated to Toni Barnhill, with thanks to God for her fervent support of my ministry and especially for her transforming ministry of the gospel in the lives of so many women. I also am grateful to the members of the session and congregation of First Presbyterian Church of Coral Springs/Margate, Fla., for their prayers, their love, and their support of my writing ministry. I also wish to thank my many friends at Ligonier Ministries and Reformation Trust, with appreciation for their work in publishing this book. I also give thanks to God for the loving companionship of my wife, Sharon, and the sacrificial support she and our children give to my labor as a minister of the gospel. I am especially grateful to Sharon for contributing the discussion questions for this book, a task at which she is considerably more gifted than I. Lastly, I give praise to God for the precious gift of His only Son, sent that we might have the priceless gift of eternal life through faith in Him.

INTRODUCTION

It says much about the importance of the gospel to Christianity that you cannot be a Christian without it.

Gospel means "good news," which is what the Christian faith proclaims to the world: the good news of salvation through God's gift of His only Son. I became a Christian because someone told me the gospel. (Actually, a number of people were involved in bringing the gospel to me, and me to it.) This activity—bringing the gospel to people—is called evangelism, so named because the Latin word for "gospel" is *evangelium*, which has come into the English language as *evangel*. One does not become a Christian by being born into a certain family, by undergoing a certain ritual, or by joining a certain organization. Christians are those who believe the gospel. Whether it is by a parent in the home, a minister in the church, or a friend in private conversation, we must be evangelized to be saved by Jesus Christ.

Furthermore, according to the four Gospels of the New Testament, the Christian faith is designed to be shared with others. The evangel is evangelistic! A true Christian church is not only evangelical, in that it holds to the biblical gospel, but it is evangelistic—it zealously spreads and shares that gospel. This means that to be a Christian is to be called as an evangelist.

But for many, this is where the difficulty sets in. As in other areas of Christianity, such as worship, preaching, and Christian discipleship, a great deal of confusion and chaos has lately surrounded the matter of evangelism. Well-intentioned Christians find themselves plagued with questions. What does it mean to be an evangelist? What does the gospel message consist of? How do I begin to talk to someone about Jesus and His offer of salvation through faith in Him? What kind of person

1

do I need to be in order to be an evangelist? And how does evangelism work—how does someone come to believe the gospel once he or she has heard it?

I would like to make the radical suggestion that the place to find answers to such questions is the Bible. Numerous training programs and aids are available to the budding evangelist today; some are fairly good and some are not. But the Christian who wishes to serve God through the spread of His gospel, and whose love for others motivates him or her to share the gospel with those who are perishing in unbelief, would be wise to begin with a study of evangelism in the Scriptures. And there is no better place to start than with the accounts of the ministry of Jesus Himself, for Jesus was an evangelist. The Bible says that Jesus went about among the people "proclaiming the gospel" (Matt. 4:23). Just as Jesus is our primary model for faith, obedience, prayer, and good works, Jesus the Evangelist should be our model for the sharing of His gospel.

While Jesus' ministry is documented and explained in many places in the Bible, the Gospel of John provides an ideal point of focus. Evangelism is the purpose of John's Gospel; as John said, "These [accounts of Jesus' ministry] are written so that you may believe that Jesus is the Christ, the Son of God, and that by believing you may have life in his name" (John 20:31).

Furthermore, John's book is distinctive in that it includes material focusing on Jesus' evangelistic ministry, accounts that are missing from the other Gospels. Primary among these are Jesus' powerful interaction with Nicodemus the Pharisee in John 3 and His conversation with the Samaritan woman in John 4. These two chapters are veritable gold mines of evangelistic instruction, revealing much of Jesus' message and method. John 1, in which Jesus' disciples are called and gathered, also provides essential insights into evangelism through the ministries of John the Baptist and of Jesus Himself.

The purpose of this book, then, is to study these key chapters from John's Gospel—chapters 1, 3, and 4—to learn evangelism from the Master

Himself. It is my hope that studying the biblical approach to evangelism afresh will help bring much-needed reform to our gospel witness.

This book is organized into three parts, corresponding to the three important chapters of John's Gospel that I have mentioned. Part 1, which covers John 1, is a study of the man who came "to bear witness about the light" (John 1:7)—John the Baptist. What did John the Baptist's witness consist of and what was important about it? This section of the book also covers the accounts of the calling of Jesus' disciples through the witness of Jesus and the disciple Andrew. The focus in these chapters is on *biblical principles for evangelism*. Why is our witness so essential? What is and what is not a good Christian witness? What are the ways in which the gospel may be witnessed? These are among the main questions answered from this part of John's Gospel.

Part 2 focuses on Jesus' remarkable encounter with Nicodemus, recounted in John 3. As Jesus interacted with this religious unbeliever—so typical of many today—He systematically presented the *theology of the gospel*. The importance of this cannot be overstated, since there must be accurate content in our gospel witness. Among the important topics that Jesus covered were the necessity of the new birth, as well as its source; God's love for the world in Christ; faith as the way of receiving God's gift; and salvation as deliverance from eternal condemnation and to eternal life. Understanding these themes as Jesus presented them is indispensable to making a clear and accurate presentation of the gospel.

Part 3 centers on Jesus' meeting in John 4 with the woman by the well in Samaria—a person very unlike Nicodemus but typical of many people today. Here we observe Jesus' *practice of evangelism* in His witness to an individual. Jesus dealt with barriers to the gospel and acted to make a personal connection. He presented His salvation offer in a way that intersected with the woman's sense of need. We witness the change that occurred in her life as her heart opened to Jesus' message. We even see the Samaritan woman responding to her belief in Jesus by sharing the gospel with others in her life.

The book concludes with an appendix dealing with a matter that troubles many people, but that ought to embolden our witness of the gospel greatly: the sovereignty of God in evangelism. I have also included discussion questions for group study, which I hope will promote personal understanding and application.

All Christians are called to evangelism. Jesus the Evangelist is our model. If we want to experience the power of God in our gospel witness, we must follow biblical principles of evangelism; we must present the true gospel in clear, scriptural terms; and we must follow Jesus' example in the practice of evangelizing actual people. Let us seek God's blessing for the salvation of many by preparing ourselves to be faithful witnesses to the gospel of God's grace.

PART ONE

The Witness of John the Baptist
and the Calling of the First Disciples:

Biblical Principles of Evangelism

Chapter 1

A Witness
to the Light

John 1:6–9

There was a man sent from God, whose name was John. He came as a witness, to bear witness about the light, that all might believe through him. He was not the light, but came to bear witness about the light. The true light, which enlightens everyone, was coming into the world.

—*John 1:6–9*

One of the most glorious works of theology ever penned is the prologue to John's Gospel. Whereas Matthew and Luke present historical accounts of the birth of Jesus, John gives us a theological account of the coming of God's Son. His message is summed up in John 1:14: "And the Word became flesh and dwelt among us, and we have seen his glory, glory as of the only Son from the Father, full of grace and truth."

But while John's prologue is theological in its content, it is historical in its progression, beginning in the infinite depths of eternity past: "In the beginning was the Word, and the Word was with God, and the Word was God. He was in the beginning with God" (John 1:1–2). Then comes Christ's role in the work of creation: "All things were made through him, and without him was not any thing made that was made" (John 1:3). The first paragraph of John's prologue concludes with a potent statement of both the person and work of Christ: "In him was life, and the life was the light of men. The light shines in the darkness, and the darkness has not overcome it" (John 1:4–5).

The second paragraph then begins to tell of the light actually coming into the world, starting with the ministry of John the Baptist, the promised forerunner and witness of the Messiah: "There was a man sent from God, whose name was John. He came as a witness, to bear witness about the light, that all might believe through him. He was not the light, but came to bear witness about the light. The true light, which enlightens everyone, was coming into the world" (John 1:6–9).

These verses remind us that John's Gospel does not merely present ideas about God, salvation, or a set of ethical principles. To be sure, Christianity does produce a philosophy and a worldview. But unlike every other religion, its truth is grounded in certain facts of history. The word *gospel* means "good news," reminding us that Christians have good tidings to tell the world—God's actions in history to save lost sinners. Something wonderful happened in the coming of Jesus Christ that we want the world to know. The purpose of John's Gospel, as with the whole New Testament, is to proclaim this good news and tell people how to be saved through faith in Jesus.

The World's Great Need

If we were to take a poll, asking people to identify the world's greatest need, the answers would be many. Some would say we must end world hunger. Others would say we need to provide education to all. Still others would suggest an end to all wars or point to the need to care for the environment, calling for an end to pollution. A famous song from the '60s said, "All you need is love," while some today look to boost self-esteem.

Starvation is a terrible problem. Lack of education keeps multitudes in ignorant darkness. War often contributes to these and other problems. There are legitimate concerns about our stewardship of the planet, and Christians should care about this. God Himself commands us to love one another, and we also should have a proper sense of self-love and dignity. But none of these issues constitutes the greatest need of this world.

What does the Bible say? As John introduces the life and ministry of Jesus Christ, it is clear what he considers to be the great need of our world: belief in Jesus Christ. John wrote his Gospel to show that "Jesus is the Christ, the Son of God, and that by believing you may have life in his name" (John 20:31).

As human beings, we are alienated from God because of our sin. God is holy, and the guilt of our sin has placed us under His just condemnation. Meanwhile, the power of sin works evil in and through our lives, so that John could say in his first epistle that "the whole world lies in the power of the evil one" (1 John 5:19). If these are our great problems—God's condemning judgment and the insidious effects of sin—the answer is the Savior whom God sent as a light to this dark world. John's most famous verse says, "For God so loved the world, that he gave his only Son, that whoever believes in him should not perish but have eternal life" (John 3:16). The true answer to the world's true problems is Jesus Christ, an answer we receive through belief in Him.

A Witness to the Light

Since our greatest need is to believe in Christ, what a blessing it is that God has sent us witnesses to Him. Such was John the Baptist: "There was a man sent from God, whose name was John. He came as a witness, to bear witness about the light" (John 1:6–7a).

The prologue to John is loaded with key terms that introduce the themes of this Gospel. John 1:4–5 reveals three of them: life, light, and darkness. Another of these theme words appears in John 1:7: *witness*. This word appears fourteen times in the Gospel of John. John's purpose in writing is to prove that Jesus is the Savior and the Son of God, and to do this he marshals an impressive array of witnesses. Through them, he seeks to multiply witnesses to Jesus—those who come to believe.

Witnesses are essential in establishing any claim to fact. When a news station wants to report an amazing event, it interviews eyewitnesses. We accept the reports of credible witnesses, especially when there are a number of them who agree. The same principle guides our legal system. When credible witnesses testify to an event, we are morally bound to accept what they say as true. In like manner, John's Gospel presents us with such witnesses to Christ. Leon Morris writes, "[John] is insistent that there is good evidence for the things he sets down. Witness establishes truth."[1] This emphasis on the validity of witnesses ought to inform our own presentation of the gospel.

What witnesses does John present? Let me list eight of them:

- First, there is the witness of God the Father. In John 8:18b, Jesus said, "The Father who sent me bears witness about me."
- Jesus, God the Son, also bore witness to Himself. He said, "If I do bear witness about myself, my testimony is true, for I know where I came from and where I am going" (John 8:14).
- Third is the witness of God the Holy Spirit, whom Jesus promised to send when He returned to heaven: "When the Helper comes, whom I will send to you from the Father, the Spirit of truth, who proceeds from the Father, he will bear witness about me" (John 15:26).
- Jesus also pointed to His works: "The works that I do in my Father's name bear witness about me" (John 10:25b). This is an important emphasis in this Gospel; John records marvelous works Jesus performed to demonstrate His deity.
- Fifth is the witness of Scripture. The most important purpose of the Old Testament was to give prophecies that would be fulfilled in Jesus; to teach God's will in a way that would be completed by Jesus; and by various means to symbolize and anticipate Jesus' coming and the salvation He would bring. Jesus said, "You search

10

the Scriptures because you think that in them you have eternal life; and it is they that bear witness about me" (John 5:39).

• One of the Old Testament's prophecies concerned a forerunner to the Messiah, whose ministry would resemble that of the prophet Elijah. This is John the Baptist, the sixth of John's witnesses.

• John's seventh witness is Jesus' disciples, including John himself. Jesus told them, "You also will bear witness, because you have been with me from the beginning" (John 15:27).

• The eighth witness is the men and women who personally encountered Jesus. One was the Samaritan woman whom Jesus met by the well. After Jesus had revealed Himself to her, she went throughout her town presenting her witness: "Come, see a man who told me all that I ever did. Can this be the Christ?" (John 4:29). Another was the man who was born blind, to whom Jesus miraculously gave sight. When the religious leaders tried to silence him, he gave this witness: "One thing I do know, that though I was blind, now I see" (John 9:25).

This is a most impressive array of witnesses to Jesus as the Son of God and Messiah. Anyone who desires to refute His claims should consider these witnesses and give careful attention to their testimony.

The prologue to this Gospel particularly stresses the witness of John the Baptist. It is appropriate that the name *John* means "the gift of God," for God gave John the Baptist to Israel as a witness to Christ: "He came as a witness, to bear witness about the light, that all might believe through him" (John 1:7). John's importance is proved by his inclusion in all four Gospels. The other three Gospels give more details of his ministry of calling the people of Israel to be baptized to show their repentance and to prepare for the Messiah. But the emphasis in John's Gospel is on the Baptist's role as a witness to Jesus. Through this witness, many of John the Baptist's disciples went on to become Jesus' disciples. Even after John had been arrested and cruelly put to death, his witness continued to bear fruit. Late in His ministry, Jesus rested in the place where John had begun his preaching ministry. So clear was John's witness that people there came to see Jesus and many believed, saying, "Everything that John said about this man was true" (John 10:41).

Three Features of a Faithful Christian Witness

John presents the eight witnesses listed above so that readers of his Gospel might believe in Jesus Christ. But another witness is essential to the work of the gospel today. This is *our* witness to the world as Christian people. The work of witnessing that Jesus gave to the first disciples now falls to us. Jesus prayed to the Father, "As you sent me into the world, so I have sent them into the world" (John 17:18). We are essential witnesses to Christ today.

By considering John's descriptions of John the Baptist, we can see three key features of a faithful Christian witness. The first has to do with the *content* of our witness. John 1:7 says that John "came as a witness, to bear witness about the light." A Christian witness is first and foremost *about Christ.*

We tell people what the early church enshrined in the Apostles' Creed: that Jesus is God's only Son and our Lord; that He was conceived by the Holy Spirit and born of the Virgin Mary; that He suffered under Pontius Pilate, was crucified, died, and was buried; that He experienced death for three days and then rose from the grave; that He ascended into heaven and sits at the right hand of God the Father Almighty; and that from there He will come to judge the living and the dead. These claims make up a Christian witness.

D. Martyn Lloyd-Jones put it this way:

> We are meant to talk to people about the Lord Jesus Christ and
> to tell them he is the Son of God and that he has come into this
> world in order to save men and women. . . . We are meant to tell
> men exactly why the world is as it is; we are meant to tell them

about sin in the human heart and that nobody and nothing can deal with it save the Son of God. . . . We are very ready to talk about our doctors, and to praise the man who cured us when so many failed; we talk about some business which is better than others, or about films and plays and actors and actresses, and a thousand and one other things. We are always glorifying people, the world is full of it, and the Christian is meant to be praising and glorifying the Lord Jesus Christ.[2]

John the Baptist set an ideal example of this. His message was not about his experiences or what he felt about God, but about Jesus. When he saw Jesus, he declared, "Behold, the Lamb of God, who takes away the sin of the world!" (John 1:29). We, too, need to declare that Jesus saves people from their sins. On the next day, "John bore witness" to Christ again, saying, "I saw the Spirit descend from heaven like a dove, and it remained on him" (John 1:32). We, too, must testify that Jesus is the One who came to do God's will by God's power. John the Baptist said, "I have seen and have borne witness that this is the Son of God" (John 1:34), and we must, too.

Second, what we read about John the Baptist should inform the *manner* of our witness. John 1:8a says, "He was not the light." It is important for us to lead lives that commend our witness to Christ, but our testimony can never be based on what good people we are or what we ourselves have to offer non-Christians. When John began his extraordinary ministry, the priests and Levites came out from Jerusalem to inquire about him. "John answered them, 'I baptize with water, but among you stands one you do not know, even he who comes after me, the strap of whose sandal I am not worthy to untie'" (John 1:26–27). With these words, John deliberately directed them away from himself and what he was doing to Jesus Christ and what He would do.

When many Christians give their witness, they talk about themselves. This is why we speak of "giving our testimonies," that is, telling people about our conversions and how Christ has helped us. There certainly is

13

a place for testimonies, but they should never form the heart of our witness. I remember seeing an ad in a secular newsmagazine that featured a handsome, smiling young man. It began by talking about his previous problems: He had been into drugs and had been lost and depressed, but now he was clean and fulfilled. The ad was like many Christian testimonies—except that it was on behalf of one of the more bizarre cults spreading today. It is true that cults can help a person get off drugs, but that does not make their beliefs true. So it is with faith in Christ; its usefulness does not prove that it is true. Moreover, it is easy for people to brush testimonies aside, saying, "I'm glad it worked for him, but that has no relevance to me." Our witness must center not on our experience but on the facts of Christ's coming to this world.

It is especially important that we never think that what we are doing for Christ is of ultimate importance. James Montgomery Boice warns us, "Whenever a Christian layman, minister, writer, teacher, or whoever it might be, gets to thinking that there is something important about him, he or she will always cease to be effective as Christ's witness."[3] We also must never permit people to glorify us for what God has done in our lives. If people notice that you have changed, you should praise God and tell them that it was Jesus' work, for they will gain what you have, not by admiring you, but only by believing on Jesus. In some cases, redirecting praise in this manner will result in people who previously admired you becoming hostile; the world hated Christ, and it will often hate a faithful witness to Him. But we must accept this risk so as to bear testimony not to ourselves but to Christ.

In John 5:35a, Jesus said that John the Baptist "was a burning and shining lamp." Some Bible versions say that John was a "light," but the Greek word Jesus used (*luxnos*) means a candle or a lamp. A lamp does not shine on its own. Its light has to be kindled from another source, and it needs a supply of oil or it will go out. The same is true of us. In our witness, we are to shine not our own light but Christ's light. Just as a lamp requires oil, we depend on our fellowship with Christ and the Holy Spirit's enlivening ministry through God's Word in order that

Christ's light may shine through us. To use a different metaphor, we are like the moon reflecting the light of the sun. On our own, we are in darkness, but a great light has shined and is shining on us, and we are to reflect it into the world.

Third, John the Baptist shows the *goal* of a faithful Christian witness. John "came as a witness . . . that all might believe through him" (John 1:7). Our goal is for others to believe through our witness. Boice writes, "It is possible for a person to become so mechanical in his witness that he can go through all the motions of witnessing without actually looking and praying for the response to Christ in faith by the other person. If we could remember this, we would find witnessing exciting, and we would learn that winning the argument often becomes far less important than winning the person to the Lord."[4] Since our goal is to persuade unbelievers and win over sinners, we should be eager to display the grace of the gospel in our lives; we should labor earnestly in prayer before and after our witness; and we should persist in telling others about Jesus even in the face of hardship and persecution. If we will commit to this pattern of faithful witness, as modeled by John the Baptist, we will find that God will cause people to believe through us. We will have the great joy of being used by the Lord for the salvation of others.

The True Light

If there is a single summary statement that should focus our witness to Jesus, it is in John 1:9: "The true light, which enlightens everyone, was coming into the world." The word *true* carries the idea of "genuine" or "real." There may be other lights in the world: ideas, products, or activities that satisfy us partially and for a time. But Jesus is the true light. No other light can show us the truth about God, about ourselves, and about life, death, and eternity. No other light can inspire us to become what we truly were meant to be or convey the power necessary to change our hearts. And no other light can guide us "in paths of righteousness" (Ps. 23:3), so that our souls arrive safely in heaven.

As I mentioned above, the great need of this world, according to John's Gospel, is that man should believe in Jesus Christ, the true light. Thus, God sent not management consultants, not psychologists, not soldiers, politicians, or stockbrokers, but witnesses to the light, so that people might believe. Believing in Christ is the world's great need, and our great obligation is to tell all people that they need to do so.

What should we tell people about Jesus today? We should tell them that their sins must be forgiven or punished by the holy God. Without the cleansing blood of a true Savior, what will they do with their sins when they die and stand before God's throne? Many expect God to admit them into heaven apart from faith in Christ because of their supposedly good lives. But have they inquired about God's actual standards? Are they willing to stake so great an issue on conventional wisdom and a fantasy spread by the world, even in the face of God's own revealed Word? The great need of men and women is to find the way God has given for forgiveness and eternal life, and our privilege is to show them the way, Jesus Christ.

I have a friend whose dying father told his Christian children that he did not think he needed Jesus because of the outstanding life he had lived. The children sent for their pastor, who came and admitted that the man had lived a virtuous life, at least as we measure such things. But then the pastor asked him, "Do you mean to tell me that you have never sinned?" The father admitted that he had committed sins, many of them, in fact. The pastor replied, "Well, what are we going to do about those sins?" With tears, the man opened his heart to Jesus, believed, and was saved.

Many people are not interested in heaven, caring only about their present happiness. But have they compared the lights of their liking to the true light of God's Son? There is no light other than Jesus that can lead to true joy now or to eternal life in days to come: not money, adventure, or success; not the pride of morality; not the pleasure of sin. The only true light is Jesus Christ, and God in His grace sent Him into this world to be our Savior. What will happen to those who reject Him? How will God respond if they do not receive His Son, bowing the knee and opening their hearts to believe and be saved? As John declared, "Whoever believes in the Son has eternal life; whoever does not obey the Son shall not see life, but the wrath of God remains on him" (John 3:36).[5]

Christians have an equal need to believe on Jesus and His gospel. Faith in Christ is once for all in its *effects*, eternally reconciling a believer to God. But faith in Christ is not a once-for-all *event*. The greatest need of Christians is to exercise their faith in Christ—to make their belief not a mere assent but a living practice and habit.

Let me provide some practical examples. What if you are taken gravely ill? You might say that your greatest need would be to receive expert medical care. That is valuable, to be sure. But the greatest need of a gravely ill Christian is to know that God holds his or her life safe for all eternity, and to experience God's loving care and the peace that only He can give. These things come only through the exercise of faith in Christ. Likewise, what is the greatest need of a Christian who gains success and worldly blessing? It is an active belief in Christ and His Word to protect him from pride and the snares of the world. A Christian facing poverty most needs, not money, but the realization that God hears his or her prayers and takes care of His own. A Christian who is lonely needs first of all the companionship of Christ. A Christian beset by temptation needs a shield of protection. A Christian who is weary needs strength and refreshment. All of these come from one and the same source: belief in Jesus Christ, in His promises, in the teachings of His Word, and in the God and Father who rules over all and who, because of His great love for us, sent the true light into the world.

Let those who wish to witness Christ to the world therefore tend to their own faith in Jesus Christ above all else. It is often the simple exercise of faith in all of life's circumstances that bears the strongest witness. Devote yourself to God's Word, the bread that feeds our faith.

Guard your faith against the many false lights in this world. Commit to a life of prayer, worship, and discipleship to Jesus, all of which depend on faith. As our faith bears its witness to the reality of Jesus, we will surely find others coming to us, as they did to John the Baptist, so that we can tell them what we know and believe.

NOTES

[1] Leon Morris, *The Gospel According to John,* revised (Grand Rapids, Mich.: Eerdmans Publishing, 1995), 66.

[2] D. Martyn Lloyd-Jones, *Safe in the World* (Wheaton, Ill.: Crossway Books, 1988), 88.

[3] James Montgomery Boice, *The Gospel of John,* 5 vols. (Grand Rapids, Mich.: Baker Books, 1999), 1:53.

[4] Ibid., 1:54.

[5] Biblical scholars disagree as to whether the words in verses 31–36 were spoken by John the Baptist or were composed by the apostle John.

Questions for discussion and reflection:

1. Today, absolute truth is "out" and relativism is "in." Many even deny that Jesus was God. What portraits of Christ from the Old Testament does John use to support claims about Jesus' deity?

2. John held the office of prophet. What evidence supports John's claims to be a true prophet, one whose message we can accept as true? Consider other people who claim to be prophets, including such people as Mohammed and Joseph Smith. Could they support their claims the way John the Baptist could?

3. Turning on a light in a dark room suddenly exposes its contents. What was and still is exposed when the light of Jesus shines in the heart of mankind?

4. What witness did Jesus bear about Himself? Commit these truths to memory and pray for the Holy Spirit to prepare you to share them with colleagues, relatives, and friends.

5. If the content of our witness is Christ, the manner is godly living, and the goal is to exhort belief, in what activities should a Christian engage to prepare to be a living witness?

6. Being enlightened by the light of Jesus is not a once-for-all event. By what means is God currently working in your life to bring about spiritual growth and to challenge you to a more authentic faith?

7. It is a privilege to intercede for one another in prayer. Who are some brothers and sisters for whom you can commit to pray, that they will be faithful witnesses to the light of Jesus Christ?

Chapter 2

THE WORD
AND THE VOICE

John 1:19–28

He said, "I am the voice of one crying out in the wilderness, 'Make straight the way of the Lord,' as the prophet Isaiah said." *John 1:23*

The October Revolution of 1917, which toppled the Russian tsar and installed the Communist regime, was chronicled by John Reed in a book titled *Ten Days That Shook the World.* Yes, the world was briefly shaken by those events. But as the years passed, the upheaval of 1917 lost its significance and the world ultimately moved on.

However, in the opening scenes of John's Gospel, we find recorded a sequence of events that truly shook the world. The seven days that began the earthly ministry of Jesus Christ will never lose their significance.

Just as Genesis 1 presents the earth's creation in seven days, John presents the coming of Christ in seven days, telling us that this was the new creation. Like the Genesis account, John presents two sections of three days each, followed by a seventh day of blessing. First are three days in which John the Baptist bore witness to Christ, followed by Jesus' first three days with His disciples. This sequence culminates on the seventh day with Jesus' first miracle, the turning of water into wine at the wedding feast of Cana. The message is that of John 1:9: "The true light, which enlightens everyone, was coming into the world."

On the first day, which is recalled in John 1:19–28, John the Baptist gave witness to a delegation of religious leaders. This is significant because it shows that witnessing always has been vital to Christianity. The early Christians understood this. Historians tell us that the astounding expansion of the church in its first centuries was due largely to the witness of every Christian. Adolf Harnack writes, "We cannot hesitate to believe that the great mission of Christianity was in reality accomplished by means of informal missionaries."[1]

In John the Baptist's witness on that first day, we can discern four key elements. They are elements that make any Christian's witness to Christ effective even today.

A Living Witness

John's first witness to Jesus was prompted by the arrival of a delegation from Jerusalem: "And this is the testimony of John, when the Jews sent priests and Levites from Jerusalem to ask him, 'Who are you?'" (John 1:19). These religious leaders came because they had heard about John and his ministry. Mark 1:4–5 describes his work and the popular response: "John appeared, baptizing in the wilderness and proclaiming a baptism of repentance for the forgiveness of sins. And all the country of Judea and all Jerusalem were going out to him and were being baptized by him in the river Jordan, confessing their sins."

John led a holy life and taught God's truth. St. Augustine says, "So great was the excellence of John, that men might have believed him to be the Christ."[2] This was borne out in the first exchange between the delegates and John: "'Who are you?' He confessed, and did not deny, but confessed, 'I am not the Christ'" (John 1:19b—20).

The delegates then put forth other guesses as to John's identity. "And they asked him, 'What then? Are you Elijah?' He said, 'I am not.'"

'Are you the Prophet?' And he answered, 'No'" (John 1:21). Based on Old Testament prophecies, the Jews thought Elijah would return before the Messiah (see Mal. 4:5). John wore garments associated with Elijah (Mark 1:6; 2 Kings 1:8), lived in the wilderness, and confronted sin just as Elijah had done. "The Prophet" was foreseen as the fulfillment of Moses' promise that God would raise up another prophet like him (Deut. 18:18). These questions from the delegates reveal the extent to which the Jews were looking for someone to deliver them again. John's life and ministry had raised hopes among the people (and concern among the religious elite) that he might be the one.

Likewise, our lives and ministries are to cause people to ask us who we are and what we represent. Peter urged believers to live exemplary lives among the pagans that "they may see your good deeds and glorify God" (1 Peter 2:12b). We will be given opportunities to witness as people observe how we live and learn what we believe. An effective witness to Jesus begins as a living witness.

Many Christians are not sure how to start witnessing. The answer is to start with the manner of your life. D. Martyn Lloyd-Jones comments:

> The first great step in evangelising is that we should start with ourselves and become sanctified. . . . When the man of the world sees that you and I have got something that he obviously has not got, when he finds us calm and quiet when we are taken ill; when he finds we can smile in the face of death; when he finds about us a poise, a balance, an equanimity and a loving, gentle quality . . . he will begin to take notice. He will say, 'That man has got something,' and he will begin to enquire as to what it is. And he will want it.[3]

There was an aged woman who credited her salvation to George Whitefield. People doubted this because she was barely old enough to have heard the great preacher from a prior age. She replied that when she was a little girl, he had stayed at her house. "It was not any sermon that he preached; it was not anything that he ever said to me," she explained. "It was the beautiful consistency and kindness of his daily life. . . . I said to myself, 'If I ever have any religion, Mr. Whitefield's God shall be my God.'"[4] Similarly, John the Baptist's life and ministry prompted his witness to Jesus, and ours must do the same.

A Witness Not to Self

In John the Baptist's answers to the religious leaders' questions, we see the second element of a successful witness. "Are you the Christ? Are you Elijah or the Prophet?" they asked him. John said, "No." John's witness was not to himself. He was not the Savior. He was not the man they should admire or trust for salvation.

It is curious that John denied that he was Elijah, because the angel who announced his birth spoke of him ministering "in the spirit and power of Elijah" (Luke 1:17). Moreover, Jesus identified John as "Elijah who is to come" (Matt. 11:14; see Matt. 17:10–13). So why did John deny that he was Elijah? One reason may have had to do with the sense in which the angel's and Jesus' prophecies were meant. John was not a reincarnation of Elijah, as some literally expected. He did not want people looking to him as the coming deliverer. But he did accept the Elijah-like role he had come to fulfill: "I am the voice of one crying out in the wilderness, 'Make straight the way of the Lord,' as the prophet Isaiah said" (John 1:23).

It is important for us to follow John's example in refusing to focus our witness on ourselves. John was a witness to the Savior, not a savior himself. This self-understanding is essential for us to remember and emulate. Our lives and ministries are to attract people's attention, but the danger is that we will allow them to admire or focus on us. People are often glad to admire our good qualities and participate in ministry events if we do not emphasize Jesus as Savior. The world is comfortable so long as we merely witness about ourselves—the good things we do and the successful techniques we employ. But these must not take the place of our witness to Christ.

Do you realize this? When you meet someone whose life needs to be straightened out, who needs to find hope, meaning, or peace, do you remember that you cannot ultimately provide these things? Certainly, you should minister as well as you can in Christ's name. But you are not the answer to any person's need, and you must not covet anyone's admiration or trust. If you really want to help someone, you must point him or her away from you or any other human minister, away from any merely human program or spiritual solution, and point to Jesus Christ, who alone can truly save.

The priests and Levites came to John, asking whether he was the Christ, Elijah, or the Prophet. John replied that they should not be focusing on him. But they kept pressing for an answer: "'Who are you? We need to give an answer to those who sent us. What do you say about yourself?' He said, 'I am the voice of one crying out in the wilderness, "Make straight the way of the Lord," as the prophet Isaiah said'" (John 1:22–23).

This should be our witness. We should say, "I am here to show that you need a Savior and to point you to the One you *should* worship and trust."

A Witness to Christ

John went on to speak about Jesus—the third element of his witness. We see this in a number of ways. First, he identified himself as "a voice." We remember that John's Gospel calls Jesus "the Word." A voice is the vehicle by which a word is made known. Jesus is the eternal Word, but He enters into our world in part through our voices. This is our pattern of witness: We are to live as lights in the world to create opportunities for witness; we are to refuse to focus attention on ourselves; and then we are to be the voices that present the Word, Jesus Christ.

As John's interview progressed, some Pharisees in the group questioned his practice of baptizing. "They asked him, 'Then why are you baptizing, if you are neither the Christ, nor Elijah, nor the Prophet?'" (John 1:25). It was understood that the Messiah's coming would involve

a cleansing. Zechariah 13:1 said, "On that day there shall be a fountain opened for the house of David and the inhabitants of Jerusalem,
to cleanse them from sin and uncleanness." But if John was not the
Messiah, Elijah, or the Prophet, what gave him the right to institute this
cleansing? "John answered them, 'I baptize with water, but among you
stands one you do not know'" (John 1:26). John showed that when we
are challenged about our right to proclaim Jesus as Savior, we must not
back down but stand upon Christ's own authority. Notice also that John
did not get tied up in a personal defense. Instead, he directed his ques-
tioners to Jesus. "The reason you ask me these things," he said, "is that
you are not aware of the One who has come." John's baptism was all
about Jesus, the true Messiah, and the religious leaders' hostility toward
John and his ministry arose from their ignorance of the Savior.

The same is true today. People are hostile to Christians because
they do not know Jesus. They do not realize the mercy He offers or the
power He gives. They do not know the glory of His character or the
faithfulness of His love. They do not understand why He died or how
He lives today. Those who do give any thought to Jesus usually picture
Him as a weak victim or an overbearing meddler. Others have heard
the truth about Him and have turned away in hardened unbelief. Jesus
was speaking of these when He said, "People loved the darkness rather
than the light because their deeds were evil" (John 3:19b). But many
people today have never once heard the truth about Jesus Christ and
His gospel. To them, He really is "One they do not know."

This means that when people argue against Christianity or teachings of the Bible, it is less important that we debate the issues than that
we tell them about Jesus. Teachings that are outrageous to the worldly
mind are made clear and lovely in the light of who Jesus is and what He
has done. For example, secular people today are incensed at the idea
that Jesus is the only Savior. But that attitude changes when they realize
that the one true and holy God sent His own Son to make a way for our
salvation at the cost of His blood! Then people stop wondering why all
sinners must come to Christ, they start wondering why anyone would

not want to come to Jesus, and they realize what an offense it is to God when they don't. The difference is all in knowing Jesus. So we should look for opportunities to talk not about the controversial teachings of the Bible, but about Jesus.

The apostle John said that Jesus is the Word made flesh (John 1:14); that He is "the true light, which enlightens everyone" (John 1:9); and that "In him was life, and the life was the light of men" (John 1:4). Such truths should always be the core of our witness. We need to tell people that while "the law was given through Moses; grace and truth came through Jesus Christ. No one has ever seen God; the only God, who is at the Father's side, he has made him known" (John 1:17–18). This is our witness: Jesus as Savior, Revealer, and Lord.

John the Baptist said, "Among you stands one you do not know, even he who comes after me, the strap of whose sandal I am not worthy to untie" (John 1:26b–27). With this obscure statement, John was saying to this delegation: "Oh, if you knew Him, you would understand. All I can really say is how great He truly is." In ancient Palestine, the roads were hot and dusty, so feet became dirty and smelly. Rabbinic writings indicate that disciples were required to perform all kinds of menial services for their rabbis, but not this! Not untying the strap of a sandal! But John said that not only was it not beneath him to perform such a menial task for Jesus, it was above him! So great is the glory of Christ![5]

Do you feel this way? Do you count it an awesome privilege to serve Jesus in any way possible? Instead of begrudging your Christian duties and especially any actual sacrifice you are called to make, are you overwhelmed at the privilege of simply serving a glorious Lord like Him? If you are not, your witness will lack power. But if you convey to people what a thrill it is to know and serve the Lord Jesus, your witness will be that much more effective.

It is interesting to note that John's witness to Jesus was not as clear as it might have been. On the very next day, he would provide a much clearer witness doctrinally. Why was this? John might have been reluctant to volunteer details to this hostile delegation. But I think it is possible that there is another explanation. According to the other Gospels, it must have been about six weeks earlier that John had baptized Jesus in the Jordan, seen the Spirit descend on Him like a dove, and heard God the Father praise Jesus from heaven. Jesus had spent the intervening time being tempted by the Devil for forty days in the desert, and was now on the brink of His return. John 1:29 says that on the day after meeting with this delegation, John saw Jesus walking by the Jordan and said, "Behold, the Lamb of God!" Until this moment, he still may have been sorting out the details of his understanding.

The application is that if you have come to Jesus as your Savior, and if you are just starting to understand His glory and grace, don't let what you *don't* know keep you from witnessing to what you *do* know. You should press on to a better doctrinal understanding of Jesus and of the gospel; this is a valuable thing. But as the Lord gives you opportunity, tell people whatever it is that you personally have learned about Christ. There is no substitute for a growing, personal relationship with Jesus. John spoke of One whom "you do not know"; this implies that John *did* know Him. Likewise, we must give not a second- or third-hand witness, but a first-hand testimony that arises from personal experience with Jesus. The more you know Jesus, the more you will not merely *give* a witness, but will *be* a witness for Him.

A Call to Repentance and Faith

Lastly, an effective witness includes a call to repentance and faith. John said he was a voice "crying out in the wilderness" (John 1:23a). A wilderness is a place of barrenness, poverty, and death. We must show people that this present life is a wilderness apart from Christ. Jesus said, "Blessed are the poor in spirit, for theirs is the kingdom of heaven" (Matt. 5:3). We must be candid with people about the real misery, emptiness, or bondage they experience. The world devotes itself to denying these things; Christians must point out the truth.

John saw himself as called to "make straight the way of the Lord"

(John 1:23). The idea behind these words is the leveling of hills and filling of holes so that the coming king might have a smooth highway. We do this for Jesus through a witness that levels the pride of unbelievers so that they become humble before Him and by showing the lost how to fill the emptiness of their hearts with faith that makes a royal way for the Savior to enter. And what about you? Do you have obstacles that are blocking Jesus' way? You should remove them, because He is the only Savior and His coming brings eternal life.

Furthermore, John's ministry of baptism called people to repent. When Gentiles wanted to join the Jewish people, they were required to be baptized as a way of confessing their sin and need of cleansing. John applied this truth not just to Gentile "outsiders" but to the whole nation of Israel itself: He called all *the Jews*, high and low, to be washed in preparation for the Lord. Likewise, we must humbly point out to people the truth that they are guilty before God, that they have broken God's law and are worthy of His just condemnation. Their greatest need is not to be washed with water; they need what baptism symbolizes—cleansing from sin by the saving work of Christ. Therefore, we need to know and tell people about the Ten Commandments so that they will be aware of their sin before God and their need to be forgiven by the blood of Christ.

Such a witness may arouse hostility. But this is the only way Jesus comes as Savior to a sinner's soul. We all must confess our sin and need, leveling our pride and lifting up our faith. This is the royal road for the King of kings. John said, "I am the voice of one crying out in the wilderness, 'Make straight the way of the Lord'" (John 1:23a). To be effective, our witness must include this same call to repentance and faith. First John 1:9 says, "If we confess our sins, he is faithful and just to forgive us our sins and to cleanse us from all unrighteousness."

No Witness Wasted

None of us is John the Baptist. He alone was the prophet called to first identify Jesus as the world's Savior. But we are called as Christians to give a witness that is *like* John's, pointing to Jesus and calling for people to open a way for Him to come into their hearts.

Perhaps the greatest obstacle to our usefulness is the false belief that our witness does not matter. This is especially a danger if we think a previous witness has been ineffective. I suppose even John might have thought that. After all, few people went to follow Jesus after John pointed him out. But there is a detail later in John's Gospel that helps us to understand better. John 1:28 says, "These things took place in Bethany across the Jordan, where John was baptizing." In John 10, we learn that Jesus at one time took His disciples back to that place: "He went away again across the Jordan to the place where John had been baptizing at first, and there he remained. And many came to him. And they said, 'John did no sign, but everything that John said about this man was true.' And many believed in him there" (John 10:40–42). Despite his apparent failure, John the Baptist's witness was not wasted; in God's timing, it led many to be saved.

One person who might think poorly of her witness is a woman whose words were instrumental in my own salvation. I do not know her name and doubt that I could recognize her. One day, as I moved into an apartment, she was moving out next door. I carried one box of books to her car. After thanking me, she asked whether I was looking for a church to attend. My body language made it clear that I did not appreciate the question. So she quickly stammered, "If you are ever looking for a church, I would recommend this particular church a few blocks away." With that, she drove off and I never saw her again. I have often imagined her kicking herself for her weak attempt to witness. But a few months later, when the Holy Spirit had prepared a way for the Lord into my heart, I remembered her words, went to that church, and, hearing the gospel there, I believed and was saved.

You may think you are just one "voice" and that your witness doesn't matter. But if Jesus is the Word your voice brings—and if He is living in you and you know Him—then your witness is mighty to cast down strongholds and lead dying sinners to salvation.

NOTES

[1] Adolf Harnack, *The Mission and Expansion of Christianity in the First Three Centuries* (New York, N.Y.: Harper & Brothers, 1961), 368.

[2] Augustine, *Homilies on the Gospel of John*, in *Nicene and Post-Nicene Fathers*, ed. Philip Schaff, 13 vols. (Peabody, Mass.: Hendrickson Publishers, 1999), 7:26.

[3] D. Martyn Lloyd-Jones, *Sanctified through the Truth* (Wheaton, Ill.: Crossway Books, 1989), 25–26.

[4] Cited from J. C. Ryle, *Holiness* (Durham, U.K.: Evangelical Press, 1979), 265.

[5] Cited from Leon Morris, *Reflections on the Gospel of John* (Peabody, Mass.: Hendrickson Publishers, 1986), 33.

Questions for discussion and reflection:

1. In what ways is the work of regeneration in a believer's life similar to God's work of Creation?

2. The content of a Christian's witness is Christ. What truths must we share about Him if we are to have a faithful and effective witness?

3. What areas of your life commend you as a witness to Jesus? What areas hinder your witness?

4. What is the danger of relying solely on a personal testimony as your witness? How can a personal testimony be used properly to support your witness to Christ?

5. John the Baptist was "the voice of one crying out in the wilderness," and we are called to play a similar role in our world today. What parallels can we draw between his ministry and our witness to Christ today?

6. If yours is to be the voice that tells people about Jesus, what passages from God's Word do you intend to use in your witness?

7. Think of an opportunity you have had to speak about Jesus. Reflecting on the content of this chapter, how would you assess the "success" of your witness?

Chapter 3

BEHOLD, THE LAMB!

John 1:29–34

The next day he saw Jesus coming toward him, and said, "Behold, the Lamb of God, who takes away the sin of the world!"   *—John 1:29*

There are times when we have to seize the moment. In football, the quarterback sees his wide receiver breaking free from the defenders and knows that the time has come to throw the ball. In romance, a young man reaches for a phone to ask a pretty girl out for dinner, knowing that the opportunity will never come again. The same is true in evangelism. God presents us with opportunities to point others to Jesus, and it is important that we know what to say when those opportunities arise.

I had this experience recently while sharing the gospel in a small town outside Kampala, Uganda. Several Ugandan Christians and I were walking through an impoverished neighborhood when we came across a group of women boiling stew on their porch. When we approached, they invited us inside their home. In some ways, it was a difficult situation. The women, along with a couple of men inside, were Muslims. Only one of them spoke English, so I had to speak with them through an interpreter. But when we brought up Jesus Christ, they were eager to talk and asked many questions. How important it was that I was able to share briefly and clearly who Jesus is and what He did for our salvation. God blessed that conversation, and it resulted in six Muslims professing faith in Jesus Christ.

Even more dramatic was the opportunity presented to John the Baptist when Jesus returned to the area where John was preaching. John had spoken of One greater than himself who would come, and now here He was. Seizing the moment, John cried out, "There He is!" As part of this important witness, John made clear and essential statements about Jesus' person and work, statements that make up Christianity's essential message of hope to the world. We need to be able to make such statements if we are to present the gospel's message of hope.

The Lamb of God

John's witness provided one of our Lord's most glorious and beloved titles: "Behold," he said, "the Lamb of God, who takes away the sin of the world!" (John 1:29).

What does it mean to say that Jesus is "the Lamb of God"? Scholars debate this, because John did not spell out his meaning. But given the background of the Old Testament, there was hardly a need for him to explain his words. If there is one prominent image in the Old Testament, it is that of the sacrificial lamb, the blood of which was shed as a symbol of the remission of sins.

Perhaps the most prominent of these images is the Passover lamb. In Exodus 12, we read of how God delivered Israel from slavery by sending the angel of death to slay all the firstborn of Egypt. Only the Israelites were offered a way of escaping this wrathful horror. Each family was to sacrifice an innocent lamb and spread its blood upon their doorposts so that the angel of death would pass over their home. There are many links between Jesus and the Passover lamb. For instance, He was handed over to be crucified at the sixth hour on "the day of Preparation of the Passover" (John 19:14). That was the very hour the Passover lambs were slain throughout Jerusalem. So calling Jesus "the Lamb of God" was

John's way of saying that His blood causes God's wrath to pass over all those who trust in Him.

This is not the only connection between Jesus and the sacrificial lambs. During the old covenant, lambs were sacrificed every day to make atonement for sin (see Ex. 29:38–39). Day by day, year by year, lambs were sacrificed in the temple as a perpetual reminder of the people's need for forgiveness. The very morning of the day when John identified Jesus as "the Lamb of God," a lamb was sacrificed, as was another that evening.

Also, naming Jesus "the Lamb of God" undoubtedly was an allusion to Isaiah 53:6, which says, "All we like sheep have gone astray; we have turned every one to his own way; and the Lord has laid on him the iniquity of us all." J. C. Ryle explains, "Christ was the great Sacrifice for sin, who was come to make atonement for transgression by His own death upon the cross."[1]

Lastly, we remember the great scene in Genesis 22, the earliest direct reference to a sacrificial lamb. At God's command, Abraham had gone up Mount Moriah to sacrifice his beloved son, Isaac. Noticing the fire and wood for an offering, the boy asked, "Where is the lamb for a burnt offering?' Abraham said, 'God will provide for himself the lamb for a burnt offering, my son'" (Gen. 22:7b–8a). Isaac's question resounds throughout the Old Testament. It is clear that a lamb must be offered to take away sin. But "where is the lamb?" People realized that no mere animal could take the place of a human in suffering the wrath of God for that person's sin, so they would have asked the priests, "Where is the true Lamb who will take away our sin?" The Old Testament comes to an end with no better answer than the one Abraham gave to his son: "God will provide the lamb."

However, on this great day beside the Jordan River, John the Baptist spied Jesus coming toward him. He raised his hand and cried aloud the great answer that was centuries in the making: "Behold, the Lamb of God, who takes away the sin of the world!"

When we understand this statement, we realize the great purpose for which Jesus came into the world. People today wonder about this. "What's the deal with Jesus?" they ask. In John's day, the people were looking for a spiritual reformer like Elijah or a deliverer like Moses to throw off the Romans. These might have been helpful, but they would not have solved the people's most fundamental problem—their need for cleansing from sin. John's witness to Jesus tells us why He came: "Behold, the Lamb of God, who takes away the sin of the world!"

Do you realize that this is what the world truly needs—to have its sins taken away and to be reconciled to God? Do you realize that this is *your* great need? Every sinner—every man, woman, or child who has broken God's holy law (and that is every one of us)—stands condemned before God's judicial wrath. By rights, God is opposed to us and not for us. Nonetheless, He loves the world, so He sent His only Son to be the Lamb to take away our sin. Ryle explains: "Christ . . . did not come on earth to be a conqueror, or a philosopher, or a mere teacher of morality. He came to save sinners. He came to do that which man could never do for himself—to do that which money and learning can never obtain—to do that which is essential to man's real happiness: He came to 'take away sin.'"[2]

How did Jesus take away our sin? By taking it on Himself and bearing our punishment upon the cross. Peter, reflecting on Isaiah 53, explains: "He himself bore our sins in his body on the tree, that we might die to sin and live to righteousness. By his wounds you have been healed" (1 Peter 2:24).

This raises the question of whose sins Jesus came to take away. Some people are confused by John the Baptist's statement that Jesus came to take away "the sin of *the world*," believing that this teaches that all people are right with God. That this was not John's meaning is evident throughout this Gospel. It is those who believe on Jesus—those who confess their sin and receive Him as Savior and Lord—who are forgiven, and only those. "For God so loved the world, that he gave his only Son, that whoever believes in him should not perish but have eternal life. . . . Whoever does not believe is condemned" (John 3:16–18a).

By speaking of "the world," John was making a contrast with the Jews. He was saying that Jesus had come to save not merely the Jews—as was believed in John's day—but also Gentiles. In short, Jesus had come to save everyone in the world who would believe in Him.

Moreover, as we study the sacrificing of lambs in the Old Testament, we see a progression that culminated with Jesus as the Lamb of God. At first, the rule was a lamb for each sinful person; this was why Abraham needed a lamb in the place of Isaac. Later, a lamb could be offered for a whole family, as in the Passover. Then, under the old covenant, a lamb could be offered for the entire nation of Israel. Finally, Jesus Christ came as the Lamb for the whole world. As He was the Son of God, His blood was of infinite worth, capable of paying the debt of every sinner.

Jesus came to save the world, and though not all sinners will repent and believe—so not all are saved—He will indeed save the world. This very world, lost and bound in sin, currently dominated and governed by unbelief, will be saved by the precious blood of the Lamb. In the end, when unrepentant sinners are cast out of this world into hell, it will be a renewed, cleansed, and sinless world that sings in praise to the Lamb: "For you were slain, and by your blood you ransomed people for God from every tribe and language and people and nation . . . and they shall reign on the earth!" (Rev. 5:9b–10).

If Jesus is "the Lamb of God, who takes away the sin of the world," then He is the Savior every sinner needs. There is no other way to be reconciled to God. In loving grace, the holy God of heaven sent His Son to die as the Lamb for our sins. What, then, will become of those who neglect, refuse, or despise this Lamb? The English poet John Donne gave an appeal that is valid still today: "Wash thee in Christ's blood, which hath this might / That being red, it dyes red soules to white."[3]

One of the famous arches in Rome celebrates the Emperor Titus' conquest of Jerusalem in AD 70. The relief on the inner curve shows Titus returning with his spoils, including the golden altar, the trumpets, and the seven-stemmed lampstand from the temple. Also shown is a long procession of Jewish slaves brought to be sold in the markets of Rome. When we look at scenes such as this, we should remember that this is what we were before the Lamb of God came for us. We were slaves to a tyrant worse than Titus. We were slaves to sin, held captive in the cruel bondage of iniquity and guilt. But now the Lamb of God has delivered us from our sin.[4] Jesus set us free and brought us into His royal family so that, with Him, we now are the victors in the battle that He won on the cross. Here is our triumph—what Christ has done as the Lamb of God for us. We simply believe on Him, committing ourselves to Him, and are saved. A healthy, spiritually thriving Christian never forgets that. He never tires of glorifying Jesus as "the Lamb of God, who takes away the sin of the world!" But he also says, "It was my sin that He took away, as well."

The Transforming Power of the Spirit

In his earlier response to the Jewish delegation, John the Baptist insisted on Jesus' total superiority over himself, and his declaration that Jesus was "the Lamb of God" also showed Jesus' supremacy. However, Christ's supremacy is further seen in John's comparison of his baptism and the baptism Jesus would bring.

John's baptism pointed out the need for forgiveness, but it was designed to point to the Savior who would actually cleanse His people from sin by His death. John said, "I came baptizing with water, that he might be revealed to Israel" (John 1:31b). Furthermore, "He who sent me to baptize with water said to me, 'He on whom you see the Spirit descend and remain, this is he who baptizes with the Holy Spirit'" (John 1:33b). With these words, God had revealed to John that the Spirit would come upon Jesus so that He would baptize not merely with water but with the Holy Spirit.

This statement attests to John's authority in making these great claims about Jesus. He was not voicing his own opinion, but witnessing to Jesus on the authority of God's revealed Word. We, likewise, must base our witness on the authority of the Bible, God's Word to us.

John's comparison of his water baptism to Jesus' Holy Spirit baptism says much about Jesus' ministry. Just as Jesus is superior because He actually takes away our sin, whereas John merely called for a confession of sin, so also Jesus is superior because He sends the Holy Spirit actually to deliver us from *the power of sin.*

By speaking of a "baptism with the Holy Spirit," John was referring to the outpouring of the Holy Spirit that would come upon the church at Pentecost after Jesus' death, resurrection, and ascension. Before returning to heaven, Jesus told His disciples, "You will receive power when the Holy Spirit has come upon you, and you will be my witnesses" (Acts 1:8a). This transformation occurred when Jesus sent His Holy Spirit to baptize the church: the disciples were empowered for holiness and for their witness to Christ and His gospel.

The power that Christians receive from the Holy Spirit deserves an important place in our witness of the gospel. Without this element, the gospel is incomplete. We will see this when we study Jesus' witness to the woman by the well. Jesus offered her "living water," and explained: "The water that I will give . . . will become . . . a spring of water welling up to eternal life" (John 4:14). Jesus was referring to the new life that comes through the Holy Spirit's indwelling. Many people are weary of the misery brought on by their sins, but it never occurs to them that life can be different. It is our privilege to tell them not only about the forgiveness that comes through the cross, but also about the life transformation that follows as the Holy Spirit brings life to our souls.

The greatest example of this transformation was the apostle Peter. At the Last Supper, when Jesus spoke about His impending arrest, Peter boasted in fleshly confidence about how faithful he would be regardless of the cost. But when the test came—when Jesus was arrested and Peter was pegged as one of His disciples—Peter betrayed the Lord. While Jesus was being crucified, Peter cowered in hiding. But after His resurrection, Jesus restored Peter. And when the Holy Spirit came upon him at Pentecost, this weak and sinful man, who so constantly misunderstood Jesus' teaching and consistently failed Him, was empowered to proclaim the gospel boldly, in the very city where Jesus had been crucified just weeks before. "This Jesus," Peter preached, "delivered up according to the definite plan and foreknowledge of God, you crucified and killed by the hands of lawless men. God raised him up, loosing the pangs of death, because it was not possible for him to be held by it" (Acts 2:23–24). God used Peter's preaching to lead multitudes to Christ, and in the years to come Peter would live for Jesus and proclaim the gospel fearlessly and faithfully.

Jesus baptized the church with the Holy Spirit so that all believers could receive this transforming power. First John 3:5 says that Jesus "appeared to take away sins." But that is not all, for a few verses later, John adds, "The reason the Son of God appeared was to destroy the works of the devil" (1 John 3:8). He is saying that Jesus came not merely to take away our guilt but to deliver us from the power of sin in our present lives. Obviously, we continue to sin—John says that if we ever think we have stopped sinning, we are only deceiving ourselves (1 John 1:8). But we do not remain slaves to sin; we no longer continue in patterns of sin. Like Peter, when someone believes and is born again, the Spirit gives him power to live in a way he never did before. Non-Christians need to be told of this new and better life.

Many New Testament passages speak of the power that comes to us from Christ and through the Spirit. For example, in John 8:36, Jesus said, "If the Son sets you free, you will be free indeed." And Paul writes, "Where the Sprit of the Lord is, there is freedom," for by the Spirit we "are being transformed into [Christ's] image from one degree of glory to another" (2 Cor. 3:17b–18b). This is good news that the world needs to hear!

If we wonder what form this transformation takes, we need look no further than the Holy Spirit's visual form as He came upon Jesus Christ. John the Baptist said, "I saw the Spirit descend from heaven like a dove, and it remained on him" (John 1:32). The dove is a symbol of purity and gentleness, which not only describes Jesus' character, but also the form the Holy Spirit's work takes in our lives. To be "spiritual"—that is, to be moved and indwelt by the Holy Spirit—is to be innocent and pure of sin's influence. Like a dove, we are to be pure and meek before God, and gentle in our dealings with other people. This is how Jesus was: He was peaceful and brought no harm. Isaiah said, "A bruised reed he will not break, and a faintly burning wick he will not quench" (Isa. 42:3). Purity, meekness, and gentleness are to characterize the Spirit-baptized church and the Spirit-indwelt Christian.

People today tend to think of these qualities—purity, meekness, and gentleness—as signs of weakness, but the Bible sees them as evidence of power. I think St. Augustine was right to associate the dove that descended on Jesus with the dove Noah sent out when the ark landed in the new world that had been cleansed by the flood. As the waters of God's wrath subsided, Noah sent out a dove, and when it returned with an olive leaf in its mouth, "Noah knew that the waters had subsided from the earth" (Gen. 8:11b). St. Augustine comments, "As a dove did at that time bring tidings of the abating of the water, so doth it now of the abating of the wrath of God upon the preaching of the Gospel."[5] Moreover, as Noah's dove signaled the arrival of a world cleansed of sin, the dove of the Holy Spirit symbolizes the new creation in Christ, the life cleansed from sin that every Christian begins when he or she trusts in Jesus Christ.

In his great hymn, "Rock of Ages," Augustus Toplady put together the dual work of Christ spoken of in John's witness. Jesus, the Lamb of God, takes away the guilt of our sin, and through His baptism with the Holy Spirit, Jesus frees us from the power of sin. This is our deliverance from sin through Jesus Christ: "Rock of Ages. . . . Be of sin the double cure / cleanse me from its guilt and power."

Trusting, Worshiping, and Witnessing to Jesus Christ

Having witnessed to Jesus' *work* as the Lamb of God and as the sender of God's Spirit, John also exalted the *person* of Christ. It is essential that our witness explain what Jesus has done for sinners, but faith ultimately looks to Jesus Himself. So what does it mean to trust in Jesus in both His person and His work?

John told us some great things about Jesus as a person. First, there were a number of implications of Jesus' title "the Lamb of God." According to the Old Testament, the sacrificial lambs had to be perfectly spotless, without any defect or blemish. This was true of Jesus: He was and is perfect in every way, especially in being pure from any taint of sin. "[God] made him to be sin who knew no sin, so that in him we might become the righteousness of God" (2 Cor. 5:21). Jesus was qualified to die in our place because He had no sins of His own for which to pay. Moreover, by calling Jesus "the Lamb of God," John pointed out His humble obedience to God's calling in His life. Isaiah said, "He was oppressed, and he was afflicted, yet he opened not his mouth; like a lamb that is led to the slaughter, and like a sheep that before its shearers is silent, so he opened not his mouth" (Isa. 53:7). Finally, because Jesus is the Lamb, He is able "to sympathize with our weaknesses" (Heb. 4:15). Thus, He is now a Shepherd who is gentle and kind to His sheep. So John proclaimed Jesus as the Lamb of God in His saving work and in His gentle ministry to us.

Jesus is altogether lovely in His person, and we need to present Him to others as such. Sometimes, when doctrinal explanations have failed to move a sinner's heart, a biblical portrait of Jesus' beautiful love will bring him or her to salvation. People are too proud to admit their sin. But seeing the person of Christ humbles them and draws them to His feet. Jesus is a kind Savior and tender minister of souls. So let us present Him in His purity, His humility, and His sympathy, and let us reveal how these virtues combined in Jesus' self-sacrifice on the cross, so that unbelieving hearts are drawn by God's Word to find their hope in Jesus.

John concluded his witness with these words: "And I have seen and have borne witness that this is the Son of God" (John 1:34). He indicated in John 1:33 that, although he knew many things about Jesus, he had not processed the whole truth until God Himself had revealed it to him when Jesus returned from the wilderness. Matthew's Gospel says that after John baptized Jesus, "a voice from heaven said, 'This is my beloved Son, with whom I am well pleased'" (Matt. 3:17). Jesus later explained that such an understanding of Him is revealed only by the Father (Matt. 16:17). This was how John the Baptist learned it. When he understood the truth, he declared, "This is the Son of God."

If Jesus' saving work calls for us to trust Him as Savior, Jesus' divine person calls for us to exalt Him as Lord. This is what we see John the Baptist continually doing. If, by God's grace, we have understood who Jesus is, we will worship and serve Him, and He will send the Holy Spirit, who strengthens us by God's Word and through prayer.

If we do exalt Jesus as Lord, there will be one last way in which we will follow the example of John the Baptist: we will tell others about Jesus. We, too, will point to Jesus and declare, "Behold, the Lamb of God, who takes away the sin of the world." To this we will add, "This is the Son of God," and we will invite others to join us in worshiping Him and trusting in Him.

Do you appreciate just how important your witness is? Jesus has come, but the world does not know Him. The world does not realize that He is the only solution to its greatest need. Once the evangelical movement was made great by its passion to spread this gospel to the farthest corners of the globe. Now, when most are unwilling even to tell their neighbors, we have become weak, and many who might be saved are lost. People cannot know Christ and His gospel unless we point Him out: "Behold, the Lamb of God!" How great is the need for these very words to be spoken in our day. May God, by the outpouring of His Spirit, cause us to bear witness to a dying world of its only Savior, "the Lamb of God, who takes away the sin of the world."

Notes

1 J. C. Ryle, *Expository Thoughts on the Gospels: John*, 3 vols. (Edinburgh, Scotland, and Carlisle, Pa.: Banner of Truth Trust, 1999), 1:56.

2 Ibid., 1:57.

3 John Donne, "La Corona," from *The Complete English Poems* (New York, N.Y.: Knopf, 1931, reprint 1985), 436.

4 Illustration cited from Jim Elliff, "The Glory of the Lamb," in *The Glory of Christ*, gen. ed. John H. Armstrong (Wheaton, Ill.: Crossway Books, 2002), 89.

5 Augustine, as cited in Ryle, *Expository Thoughts on the Gospels: John*, 1:65.

Questions for discussion and reflection:

1. Read Exodus 12. Why did God have the Israelites place blood on the doorposts? Where did that blood come from? What happened to those homes where no blood was present?

2. John the Baptist described Jesus as "the Lamb of God." How were the Old Testament lamb offerings similar to Jesus' atoning work? What was the key difference in Jesus' sacrifice?

3. The greatest need of every person is the forgiveness of his or her sins and reconciliation to God. How did Jesus accomplish this for us?

4. The doctrine of the Trinity is powerfully portrayed in John 1. God the Father sent Jesus to die, and Jesus then sent the Holy Spirit. If Jesus' sacrifice was sufficient and complete, why do believers need the ministry of the Holy Spirit?

5. How does your life reflect the transforming power of the Holy Spirit?

6. Identify one area in which you need to grow spiritually. Pray for the Spirit's ministry in your life and others' lives, that He might increasingly conform you to Christ.

Chapter 4

BRINGING THEM
TO JESUS

John 1:35–42

Jesus turned and saw them following and said to them,
"What are you seeking?" And they said to him, "Rabbi"
(which means Teacher), "where are you staying?" He said
to them, "Come and you will see." So they came and saw
where he was staying, and they stayed with him that day.

—*John 1:38–39a*

Some of the most valuable Christians are not those with the
greatest gifts, but those who bring gifted people to Christ. One
example is an English monk who was nicknamed "Little Bilney"
because of his short stature.

Bilney had been influenced by Martin Luther's books and was an
early promoter of the Protestant Reformation. He realized that he was
not well-educated or greatly gifted, but he had noticed a priest named
Hugh Latimer who possessed great learning and ability. Bilney began
praying about how he might witness the gospel to Latimer, and came
up with a strategy. Priests were required to hear confessions of sins. So
one day, Bilney went to Latimer, tugged at his sleeve, and asked him to
hear his confession. After they entered the booth, Bilney confessed the

gospel. He told Latimer that he was a sinner and knew his good works could not save him. But he also confessed that Jesus had died for him and that, through faith, the righteousness of Christ had been imputed to him apart from good works. Hearing this confession of the gospel, Latimer was converted. He became one of the great preachers of the English Reformation, and his martyrdom for Christ was one of its great inspirations. It all began with Little Bilney, who, though short in stature and little known to history, did much for the kingdom of Christ.[1]

There is always much discussion as to the best method of evangelism. Some emphasize a very direct approach, in which people—even strangers—are addressed with the aim of discussing their eternal salvation. Others stress a more relational approach, in which Christians seek to establish a personal connection, out of which might grow a receptivity to the gospel. Some people prefer to hand out tracts or other printed material, and others engage in open-air preaching. In my opinion, there is a great need for all of these methods of evangelism. Instead of picking and choosing between them, we can best profit by considering all of these approaches and making use of them as God gives us opportunity.

In John 1:35–42, we see elements of each of these approaches. The apostle relates three witnesses that occurred on the third and fourth days of the first week of Jesus' ministry. One was given by John the Baptist, as he proclaimed the biblical message of Jesus. The second was given by Andrew, as he told what he had learned and experienced of Jesus, just as Bilney later did for Latimer. The third was given by Jesus Himself, as He extended a personal invitation to some of John the Baptist's disciples to "come and see."

John the Baptist's Witness: Biblical Proclamation

The apostle John begins by reporting the witness of John the Baptist: "John was standing with two of his disciples, and he looked at Jesus as he walked by and said, 'Behold, the Lamb of God!'" (John 1:35–36).

John is a great example to us in evangelism. Being a prophet, he gave his testimony in public, calling all people to repent and believe that the Savior had come. John is also outstanding in that he was not interested in acquiring followers for himself; his chief desire was to direct others to follow Jesus Christ.

Above all, John is a strong example of the use of *biblical proclamation* in our witness. Many Christians wonder what to say to others about Jesus. John shows that we should always be ready to state what the Bible says about Him. For instance, someone might ask, "What is it about Jesus that so fascinates you Christians?" You could then reply, "The Bible says that Jesus is the Lamb of God, the sinless Savior who died for our sins." From there you might go on to explain more of the gospel. Or, given the opportunity, you might make note of the famous "I am" sayings in the Gospel of John—Jesus said He is the bread of life; the light of the world; the door of the sheep; the good shepherd; the resurrection and the life; the way, the truth, and the life; and the true vine. You might point these out in the Bible and explain what they say about Jesus. I once taped these seven "I am" sayings to the inside cover of a Bible to help me witness, and I found them to be extremely effective.

Another famous approach to proclaiming the gospel is the so-called "Romans Road." This is a short-hand way of following Paul's gospel proclamation in the book of Romans. You start by stating that "all have sinned and fall short of the glory of God" (Rom. 3:23). Next comes the statement that "the wages of sin is death, but the free gift of God is eternal life in Christ Jesus our Lord" (Rom. 6:23). You then explain how salvation happens by reading, "God shows his love for us in that while we were still sinners, Christ died for us" (Rom. 5:8). The question then is "How can that be true for me?" You answer, "If you confess with your mouth that Jesus is Lord and believe in your heart that God raised him from the dead, you will be saved. . . . For everyone who calls on the name of the Lord will be saved" (Rom. 10:9–13). When I was first converted, I marked the pages where those passages were found so that I could have others follow the Romans Road for themselves.

We need to have this kind of biblical proclamation ready at hand so that we can tell people what the Bible says about Jesus. We may have to repeat these things, as John the Baptist repeated his witness to Jesus as the Lamb of God. But we should always emphasize the actual teaching of the Bible in our witness, because it is the Word of God that brings people to faith. Peter wrote to believers, "You have been born again . . . through the living and abiding word of God" (1 Peter 1:23), so we need to witness to Jesus by presenting the Bible's teaching about Him.

Andrew's Witness: Personal Testimony

The second witness we see is Andrew's. Andrew is usually listed as one of the first four disciples (see Matt. 10:2; Mark 3:16–18; and Luke 6:14), but he is much less known than the other three: Peter, James, and John. Andrew's contribution was similar to that of Little Bilney. He is most noted for bringing people to Jesus: all three times he is singled out in John's Gospel, it is for this reason. In our passage, he brought his brother Simon to Jesus. Later, when Jesus wanted to feed the five thousand, it was Andrew who brought the boy with five barley loaves and two fishes to Jesus (John 6:8–9), and shortly before Jesus' death, Andrew and Philip together brought a group of Greeks who wanted to meet the Lord (John 12:20–22). Peter might be called "the Rock," James and John might be dubbed "the Sons of Thunder" (Mark 3:17), but Andrew's notoriety is the most excellent of all—he was the one who brought people to the Savior.

Andrew's example is instructive for the topic of evangelism. First, we note his willingness to take a back seat if only he could bring others to the Lord. John MacArthur writes: "[Andrew] did not seek to be the center of attention. He did not seem to resent those who labored in the limelight. He was evidently pleased to do what he could with the gifts and calling God had bestowed on him, and he allowed the others to do likewise."[2] Those who are greatly concerned about their own place and the importance of their own ministry are seldom effective evangelists.

Like Andrew, we must desire most of all for people to come in faith to Jesus Christ.

Next, we note Andrew's zeal to share what he had found in Jesus. John 1:41 says, "He first found his own brother Simon." The first thing Andrew did was witness to his brother. Many of us find it hard to speak about our relationship with Jesus to those who are closest to us. It is a sad reality that many Christians do not witness to their relatives and closest friends. But Andrew was too zealous for that to be true of him. It was the very first thing he did after he left Jesus' presence.

This is how it ought to be with new converts—they should not be able to restrain themselves from talking about Jesus. But the same should be true for every Christian: Our excitement about the Lord should create a zeal to share what we have found. For many of us, Andrew's example provides a much-needed rebuke. Alexander Maclaren writes: "This man, before he was four-and-twenty hours a disciple, had made another. Some of you have been disciples for as many years, and have never even tried to make one."[3] If that is even partly true of you, you should ask why, then draw near to Jesus for forgiveness and for a love for others that will make you more like Andrew.

Andrew's witness to Peter took the form of a *personal testimony*: "We have found the Messiah" (John 1:41). Our witness should always include a biblical explanation about Jesus, but it is also important for us to speak of our own experience with the Lord. Peter knew what *Messiah* meant. John tells his Greek readers that this term means "the Christ"— that is, the "Anointed One" who would come to save and lead Israel. But Andrew also shared his personal experience. Maclaren comments, "The mightiest argument that we can use, and the argument that we can all use, if we have got any religion in us at all, is that of Andrew, 'We have found the Messiah.'"[4]

What kind of things should we tell others about Jesus? We should tell them what caused us to believe. We should tell what we have experienced in our hearts: the joy of knowing our sins are forgiven, the peace that comes through the Holy Spirit, the love we feel as children of God, and the excitement of seeing the truth with new eyes. If you have a good doctor, you tell your friends that they should see him when they are sick. Are your friends not sick in their souls? If you find a store with a great sale, you call your family members and friends to let them know. But here are blessings that money cannot buy—blessings that are, in fact, available to all by God's free gift of grace—and that never perish or fade. We should tell people what it has meant to us to turn away from sins that had dragged us down for so long, and to have a power within that enables us to walk in faith with God.

A personal testimony does not replace a biblical proclamation about Jesus, but it is an important complement. And it requires that we have a close relationship with the Lord. If we are not excited about God's Word, if we are not warmed by close fellowship with God, and if we are not humbled by Christ's suffering on the cross for our sins, we will not be very effective witnesses. Yet it is essential that we be able to give such a witness. MacArthur is right when he says:

> Most people do not come to Christ as an immediate response to a sermon they hear in a crowded setting. They come to Christ because of the influence of an individual. . . . In the overwhelming majority of [new believers' testimonies], they tell us they came to Christ primarily because of the testimony of a coworker, a neighbor, a relative, or a friend. . . . There's no question that the most effective means for bringing people to Christ is one at a time, on an individual basis.[5]

Between these two brothers—Peter and Andrew—we see the two main kinds of witnesses God provides in the church: the public preaching of the Word and the personal testimony of individual Christians. Every church needs a Peter who will preach the gospel publicly, and God greatly uses faithful preaching. Peter's sermon at Pentecost, when three thousand people believed on Christ, is one such example. But as important as preaching is, it is at least as necessary that a church have a legion of Andrews: those who bring people to Jesus one by one through their heartfelt testimonies.

When you lead someone to Jesus, it may be that God will use that person in a mighty way. That was the case with Andrew; his bringing Peter to Jesus was a great moment in Christian history. Another such example was the witness of Edward Kimball to a shoe salesman he had met. Kimball was a timid, soft-spoken man—the very opposite of a bold evangelist—while the shoe salesman was a crude and illiterate person. But God laid it on Kimball's heart to speak with the salesman about Jesus. So Kimball headed to the shoe store, uncertain whether he should be going there during business hours and unclear as to what he would say. He was so preoccupied that he walked right past the store, but realizing this he determined to get his mission over with and dashed right in. He found the young man shelving shoes in the stockroom. As Kimball later remembered it, he spoke with "limping words": "I never could remember just what I did say: something about Christ and His love; that was all." It was, in his judgment, "a weak appeal," but God used his witness so that the young man gave his heart to Jesus Christ.[6]

This was a memorable event because that shoe salesman was Dwight L. Moody, who went on to be one of the greatest evangelists in history. Moody's ministry had a massive impact in America and in Britain. He founded the famous Moody Bible Church in Chicago, along with the Moody Bible Institute, from which the gospel is heard today on the Moody Christian radio network. Millions of people have been reached over the decades through the ministry of Dwight L. Moody, once an illiterate unbeliever, and it all began when one Christian man was faithful to bring another person to Jesus.

That is what Andrew did, and that is what we are all called to do. I have noted that Andrew is overshadowed in the Bible by more famous disciples such as Peter, James, and John. But there are no more glorious words written about anyone in the Bible—apart from Christ—than the words spoken of Andrew in John 1:42a: "He brought him to Jesus."

If we really care about people—especially those closest to us—then it should be our most fervent prayer and most ardent desire that this could be said of us as well: "He brought them to Jesus."

The Witness of Jesus: His Personal Invitation

I noted that there are three witnesses in this passage. The third comes in the form of a *personal invitation* from Jesus Christ. Jesus saw the two disciples of John coming to Him and asked, "What are you seeking?' And they said to him, 'Rabbi . . . where are you staying?' He said to them, 'Come and you will see'" (John 1:38b–39a). This is a great invitation to all people: "Come and you will see." With those words, Jesus invites everyone to discover personally the Savior that He is and shows us a vital element for our own witness.

Jesus' invitation to the disciples of John was couched in the form of a promise: "If you come, you will see." This promise is still valid today. If a man or woman will sincerely seek to learn about Jesus, He will show that person who He is. Many times I have suggested to someone who was not certain about Jesus that he or she should read the Gospel of John, sincerely seeking to learn about Jesus. Time after time, I have later found that the person came to Jesus and that He *did* reveal Himself to that individual's heart, so that he or she became His disciple.

Stan Telchin was a traditional Jewish father whose daughter, Judy, informed him that she had come to faith in Christ. A friend at college had given her a Bible and helped her to study it, with the result that she believed. Despite knowing that her family would be bitterly opposed to her conversion, Judy nonetheless spoke to her father in words similar to those used by Andrew in his witness to his brother Simon. She said, "I believe that the Bible is the Word of God, and I believe that Jesus is the Messiah."[7] Then she gave her parents New Testaments, saying, "Read the Bible for yourself and find out whether it's true or not."[8] Judy combined all three kinds of witnesses we have studied: biblical proclamation about Jesus, her personal testimony, and Jesus' own invitation.

Stan felt utterly betrayed. Judy's conversion to Christ was worse than if she had gotten pregnant or been kicked out of school! But he loved his daughter, and he and his wife could not help noticing the positive changes in her life. So he took up her challenge to read the Bible, determined to prove her wrong. Instead, he found that Jesus' invitation is true. As he studied the Bible, his eyes were opened by the Lord and he saw for himself that Jesus is the Messiah. He went on to have a powerful evangelistic outreach to other Jews, and Stan and his book *Betrayed!* have been used to lead many Jews to Jesus.

If you will come to inquire about Jesus, honestly seeking in the Bible who He is and what He has to offer, this will happen to you. You will be faced with the power of God's truth in the good news of salvation. If you seek Jesus, He will reveal Himself to you by the ministry of the Holy Spirit, as He illuminates the Scriptures to your mind and heart. If you find that hard to believe, take Jesus at His word: "Come," He says, "and you will see." And when you find Him, you also will find a new life with God, a life of light, love, and truth.

God calls us to deliver this very invitation to the multitudes around us. We do not need to coerce them into making a profession of faith. Rather, we set the truth of Jesus before them, pray for God's working, and encourage them to believe. On many occasions, I have concluded a gospel witness by presenting a Bible, with some advice on where to read (often, it is the Gospel of John). I have encouraged my hearers to read about Jesus for themselves and to ask God to reveal the truth to their hearts. The psalmist said, "Taste and see that the Lord is good!" (Ps. 34:8), and this is a good witness. Often, having had their appetite whetted by a sincere Christian witness, people go on to read the Bible and find themselves coming to Jesus and gaining His salvation.

Bringing Them to Jesus

What a blessing it is for believers to have these simple and straightforward examples of Christian witness. There is John the Baptist, who boldly proclaimed the biblical testimony regarding Jesus Christ. Every Christian should be able to lead another person through the biblical teaching regarding Jesus simply and directly. Peter wrote in his first epistle, "Always [be] prepared to make a defense to anyone who asks you for a reason for the hope that is in you" (1 Peter 3:15b). Christianity is not a blind leap into darkness; we are to believe based on the compelling witness of the Scriptures, and we who do believe are to be able to present that witness to others.

Then we have the witness of Andrew, who is a model to us all in so many ways. Like him, we must take an interest in individual people. Jesus builds His church one person at a time through the kind of relationship evangelism Andrew modeled. We must experience the blessings of the Lord for ourselves, and then we must simply and caringly share what we have experienced of Jesus with others.

Last, and most important, we must realize that Jesus stands before the world today, just as He did in the time of those first disciples. He still is calling men and women with His gospel invitation. He says, "Come to me, all who labor and are heavy laden, and I will give you rest" (Matt. 11:28). He cries out: "If anyone thirsts, let him come to me and drink. Whoever believes in me, as the Scripture has said, 'Out of his heart will flow rivers of living water'" (John 7:37b–38). He teaches: "I am the way, and the truth, and the life. No one comes to the Father except through me" (John 14:6).

Therefore, our witness must always have this aim: not to win arguments, not to present an interesting philosophy or a helpful lifestyle, but to bring people to Jesus. He is the only One who truly can save the sinner's soul, and if we simply bring people to Him, He will do the rest. "The Son of Man came to seek and to save the lost," Jesus said (Luke 19:10). He is seeking and saving the lost today just as in prior times, and He does so through our witness that brings people to Him.

Can that happen through your witness? Yes! Andrew brought Peter, and Jesus saved him. Little Bilney entered the confessional booth and spoke of the cross to a high-minded scholar, and Jesus saved Hugh

Latimer. Edward Kimball stammered about Christ's love in the back room of a shoe store, and Christ made an evangelist for Himself. Judy Telchin tearfully told her Jewish father that she had found the Messiah, and through his love for her and her challenge to seek the truth, Stan Telchin found the Savior, too. It is not our witness that saves. But we must witness! And if we will only bring them to Jesus, He is the Savior who will grant salvation.

Notes

1. Cited in James Montgomery Boice, *Acts: An Expositional Commentary* (Grand Rapids, Mich.: Baker Books, 1997), 316.

2. John MacArthur, *Twelve Ordinary Men* (Nashville, Tenn.: Thomas Nelson, 2002), 63.

3. Alexander Maclaren, *Expositions of Holy Scripture*, 17 vols. (Grand Rapids, Mich.: Baker Books, 1982), 10:64.

4. Ibid., 10:67.

5. MacArthur, *Twelve Ordinary Men*, 68–69.

6. Ibid., 69–70.

7. Stan Telchin, *Betrayed!* (Grand Rapids, Mich.: Chosen Books, 1981), 12.

8. Ibid., 22.

Questions for discussion and reflection:

1. What does the example of Little Bilney teach us about evangelism? How does it inspire us in our personal witness?

2. John the Baptist exemplifies biblical proclamation in our witness to Christ. What Bible verses or passages have enabled you to communicate the message of Jesus effectively? Consider committing to memory a series of Bible verses that summarize the gospel effectively.

3. Andrew is famous for bringing people to Jesus. Is there at least one person for whose salvation you are praying? If God gives you an opportunity to witness to this person, what do you plan to do?

4. Share your experiences in witnessing to family members or close friends. What made this difficult? What enabled you to present a clear witness? If you have not been willing to share the gospel with those close to you, why do you think that is? What fears or anxieties are hindering your witness to relatives and friends?

5. Have you ever taken the time to consider your personal testimony? Are you able to explain what it has meant to you to know the grace of Jesus Christ? Reflecting on the material in this chapter, take some time to write out your personal testimony of the blessings you have received from Christ.

6. How can you encourage or challenge a skeptic to give serious consideration to the Bible's teaching about Jesus? What insights do you gain from the example of Judy Telchin?

7. What are some of the fears and anxieties that most inhibit your witness to Jesus? Pray for yourself and others, that you might have boldness to share the most important good news that people you love need to hear.

PART TWO

Jesus' Witness to Nicodemus:

The Theology of the Gospel

Chapter 5

BORN AGAIN

John 3:1–8

> Jesus answered him, "Truly, truly, I say to you, unless one is
> born again he cannot see the kingdom of God." —*John 3:3*

John's account of Jesus' visit to Jerusalem at the beginning of His ministry is brief (2:13–25). Jesus went up for the Passover and found merchants doing business in the temple. He made a whip of cords and drove them out, provoking His first confrontation with the religious leaders. John concludes: "Many believed in his name when they saw the signs that he was doing. But Jesus on his part did not entrust himself to them, because he knew all people and needed no one to bear witness about man, for he himself knew what was in man" (John 2:23b—25).

This is the background for the meeting of Jesus and Nicodemus. John says, "Now there was *a man* of the Pharisees named Nicodemus" (John 3:1). It would have been easier for John to write, "Now there was a Pharisee. . . ." Instead, he wrote, "Now there was a man of the Pharisees." The connection is clear: "Jesus knew what was in a man. . . . Now there was a man." Nicodemus represents those who possess a certain belief in Jesus, or at least a certain regard for Him, but one which Jesus neither accepts nor embraces.

John 1 presents rich material offering principles for evangelism.

In John 3, which we will study in the next four chapters of this book, we witness Jesus engaging in an intense evangelistic encounter. Jesus' handling of Nicodemus gives us additional insights into our approach to unbelievers—especially to unbelievers of Nicodemus's proud kind. But of special interest in this encounter is Jesus' explanation of the theology of the gospel, which we must understand if we are to help others come to grips with their need to embrace Jesus as Savior and Lord.

Nicodemus the Man

In our study of evangelism, it is important for us to understand Nicodemus, as well as Jesus' witness to him, because he represents so many people today. We can readily discern three things about him, beginning with his identity as a Pharisee.

The Pharisees were a sect of men, never numerous, who lived above the common level of life. People today do not think highly of them because of Jesus' criticism of their self-righteous hypocrisy. However, they were the most respected people of their time. Jesus' problems with the Pharisees stemmed from their religious practice and teaching, but it could not be denied that they were exceedingly moral. Such a man was Nicodemus, an exemplar of moral conduct.

Second, Nicodemus was a leader in Israel. He was "a ruler of the Jews" (John 3:1), a member of the Sanhedrin, the highest governing body. Therefore, Nicodemus was a member of the ruling elite.

Third, it is most likely that Nicodemus was a scholar. All Pharisees were devoted students of Scripture. It is noteworthy, as well, that *Nicodemus* is a Greek name. Upper-class Jews often gave their children both Jewish and Greek names, signifying the two worlds in which they traveled. Nicodemus may have chosen to adopt his Greek name because he was an admirer of the philosophers.

So Nicodemus was not merely a man—he was quite a man. It is hard to pick a similar figure from our own time, one who combines political power with moral excellence and erudite scholarship. If religious mankind were to have had a representative in Jerusalem, there hardly could have been a better one than Nicodemus.

Like Jesus, we also will have opportunities to share the gospel with the "better kind" of people, that is, with people who enjoy wide admiration and thus may never have considered their need for a Savior. But they need Jesus! By observing Jesus' interaction with Nicodemus, we can learn much about our witness to such men and women.

Undercover Evangelism

Why did a man like this come to see Jesus? John records: "This man came to Jesus by night and said to him, 'Rabbi, we know that you are a teacher come from God, for no one can do these signs that you do unless God is with him'" (John 3:2). By his own words, Nicodemus indicated that he had seen something of Jesus' power in His miracles, had become intrigued, and wanted to meet Him. In the same way, people like Nicodemus will come to us if Jesus' power is evident in our lives.

Nicodemus came under cover of darkness. Evidently he did not want his fellow Pharisees and power-brokers to know of this meeting, perhaps for fear of embarrassment. Honest discussions with religious unbelievers often take place this way.

Such unbelievers frequently are patronizing in their approach to Jesus and the Bible. "Rabbi," Nicodemus began, "we know that you are a teacher come from God." There is, I believe, more than a hint of patronization in these words. "We know," he said, making Jesus aware that he was speaking for powerful others who had condescended to give him a favorable report. I don't think it is too much to suggest that Nicodemus meant to impress upon Jesus the strength of his position and resources. Such things are important to the religious unbeliever. Nicodemus might have gone on to remark: "We know you are from God. But things are much different in Jerusalem than way out in Nazareth. You are going to need good advice, handling, support, and resources. We can guide you in your affairs." Jesus cut Nicodemus off before he could say such things, but what he did say suggests a patronizing attitude toward our Lord.

According to Nicodemus, he knew that Jesus was "a teacher come from God." That was all. He reminds us of the many people who compliment Jesus so long as He remains just a teacher. How different this is from those who are commended in Scripture for true faith, who come to Jesus crying, "Lord, have mercy on us!" Nicodemus may have come to Jesus with good will, but his approach was that of an equal or a patronizer, not that of a believer in his Savior or a worshiper before his God.

"You Must Be Born Again"

It is significant that Jesus did not welcome Nicodemus's advance. Had Jesus been a mere teacher, a mere man, these words would have been music to His ears. He was being recognized, accorded access, and promised support! But Jesus bluntly stated that Nicodemus did not know what he was talking about. Indeed, he could not know. "Truly, truly, I say to you," Jesus replied, "unless one is born again he cannot see the kingdom of God" (John 3:3).

A comparison of others' encounters with Jesus helps us to see this as the reproof it was. To the rich young ruler, so devoted to his money, Jesus commanded, "Sell what you possess and give to the poor" (Matt. 19:21). To the woman at the well, He offered "living water" (John 4:10). Jesus always directs us away from our worldly sources of confidence to the spiritual realities of heaven. So to the confident Pharisee, who was so proud of his lineage, He said, "You must be born again" (John 3:7). Leon Morris observes, "In one sentence he sweeps away all that Nicodemus stood for, and demands that he be remade by the power of God."[1] We can learn from this reproof to think about what false sources of confidence people we know are relying upon. These are pressure points where we should prayerfully apply the challenges of God's Word.

It is not just Nicodemus who needs to be born again. What Jesus told him is true for all people: We "must be born again." This is one of the great statements of the Bible. Jesus said that salvation requires not a superficial change, temporary religious excitement, or a grasping of new ideas. We cannot just fix the old person or clean up our acts. Salvation requires a radical revamping by which we are made inwardly new. J. C. Ryle explains: "It is a thorough change of heart, will, and character. It is a resurrection. It is a new creation. It is a passing from death to life. It is the implanting in our dead hearts of a new principle from above."[2]

This is, no doubt, one of many occasions when the apostle John intentionally uses a word that conveys a double meaning. The expression *born again* also can be translated as "born from above." The Greek word *anothen* combines the adverb "above" with the suffix "from." It is found five other times in the New Testament, including verse 31 of this chapter, and in each of those occasions it is translated as "from above." The new birth is a birth "from above." This is the point John makes in his prologue when he says that those who receive Jesus become children of God, born "not of blood nor of the will of the flesh or nor of the will of man, but of God" (John 1:12–13). The new birth Jesus is talking about is from above, that is, from God.

Nonetheless, Nicodemus's response revealed that he took Jesus' meaning to be "born again," which *anothen* can also mean. "How can a man be born when he is old?" he asked in response to Jesus' statement. "Can he enter a second time into his mother's womb and be born?" (John 3:4).

Jesus answered: "Truly, truly, I say to you, unless one is born of water and the Spirit, he cannot enter the kingdom of God" (John 3:5). What does Jesus mean by "born of water and the Spirit"? Some believe *water* refers to baptism and *Spirit* refers to conversion. The problem with this view is that there is nothing here to indicate that *water* refers to baptism. Moreover, the Bible does not teach that true spiritual change results merely from undergoing any ritual, but instead speaks of the new birth as resulting from God's Word (see 1 Peter 1:23). Another view holds that *water* and *Spirit* describe two different births—one from a mother's womb by water and the other a supernatural birth by the Spirit. Jesus' words in John 3:6 are thought to support this view: "That which is born of the flesh is flesh, and that which is born of the Spirit is spirit." But this is not the best view, since in the Greek text the grammatical structure of "water and the Spirit" indicates a single event, not two different births.

The third and best view takes into account that Jesus chided Nicodemus for his ignorance (John 3:10). So He must be referring to things taught in the Old Testament. It turns out that Jesus' description of the new birth as being by "water and the Spirit" corresponds to God's promise of the new birth in Ezekiel 36:25–27: "I will sprinkle clean water on you, and you shall be clean from all your uncleannesses, and from all your idols I will cleanse you. And I will give you a new heart, and a new spirit I will put within you. And I will remove the heart of stone from your flesh and give you a heart of flesh. And I will put my Spirit within you, and cause you to walk in my statutes and be careful to obey my rules."

This is a rebirth that a Bible teacher like Nicodemus should have known. It involves cleansing from sin as by water, giving us a new and righteous standing with God, and the transforming of the heart by God's Spirit, giving us new power to live for God. This is what the new birth is all about.

Jesus' Teaching on the New Birth

We can summarize Jesus' teaching on the new birth in three points: It is *necessary*, it is a *supernatural work of God,* and it is *revealed by its effects.*

Twice in this passage, Jesus said, "Truly, truly, I say to you," words that indicated the importance of what He was teaching. This underscored His point that the new birth is *necessary*: "You *must* be born again" (John 3:7, emphasis added). Until God regenerates us—that is, brings us to spiritual life—we are not even interested in God, Jesus, or salvation. If we hear the gospel in this unregenerate state, it makes no impact on us, and to the extent that we understand it, we dislike it. Instead, we are attracted to worldly and sinful things. "That which is born of the flesh is flesh," Jesus said, "and that which is born of the Spirit is spirit" (John 3:6). Until people are born again, they do not want to read the Bible and do not accept what it says, just as the spiritually dead people of Jesus' time rejected and crucified Him. D. Martyn Lloyd-Jones explains:

> The world is not interested in the affairs of the soul at all and tries to avoid considering them. The world is spiritually dead, dead in trespasses and sins and it regards spiritual things as utterly boring. It wants to enjoy the world, it is out for the glittering prizes that the world has to offer. But the Christian has been made spiritually alive. He is very concerned about the affairs of the soul, they are the things that come first in his life and in all his thinking. How . . . has this happened? It is the power of Christ that has come upon him: "God has made us alive with Christ even when we were dead in transgressions" (Eph. 2:5).[3]

The Bible says that before we are born again, we are spiritually dead (Eph. 2:1). A dead person cannot believe or act in any way to save himself; he must be made alive. Like Lazarus in the tomb, he must hear the voice of Jesus—only then can he come forth and live. Not only that, before being born again, we are spiritually blind. Jesus said the new birth is necessary not merely to enter the kingdom of God (John 3:5), but even to see it (John 3:3).

Nicodemus is an example of this. He began by talking about all that he and his colleagues knew. But not having experienced the rebirth of the Holy Spirit, he knew nothing of spiritual things. He may have been vastly learned—and learning is a good thing—but because God apparently had not given him a new heart and a new light in the mind, he could not grasp the things of heaven. Paul explains why: "The natural person does not accept the things of the Spirit of God, for they are folly to him, and he is not able to understand them because they are spiritually discerned" (1 Cor. 2:14). Therefore, Charles H. Spurgeon writes, "Ye may be rich or ye may be poor, but 'ye *must* be born again.' Ye may be intelligent, ye may be educated, ye may be talented, but 'ye *must*, ye *must* be born again."[4]

The second point in Jesus' teaching is that the new birth is not something we do for ourselves but is a *supernatural work of God*. This is seen in the terminology *born from above*. Just as we do not bring about our own natural births, so spiritual rebirth is not our doing. It is the work of God's grace; salvation is His gift. Morris observes, "Entry into the kingdom is not by way of human striving, but by that rebirth which only God can effect."[5]

Nicodemus was puzzled by the idea of being reborn. He asked, "How can a man be born when he is old? Can he enter a second time into his mother's womb and be born?" (John 3:4). He was thinking of ways in which a man might cause himself to be born again. But Jesus insisted that only the Holy Spirit can cause the new birth: "That which is born of the flesh is flesh, and that which is born of the Spirit is spirit" (John 3:6). Skip Ryan explains: "Being born again is not a decision you make. Whoever you are, however you came to Christ, you have been the object of God's supernatural work on your heart."[6]

These two observations remind us of the importance of prayer to the work of evangelism. When we witness the gospel to unbelievers, we are speaking to spiritually dead men and women. This fact should not deter us, but it should cause us to realize the limitations of our own efforts. The new birth is God's supernatural work, so we must rely on His gracious activity. Realizing this will bring us to our knees when we think about sharing the gospel with sinners, and during our evangelism it will motivate numerous silent prayers. Moreover, when we recognize that only God can grant the new birth, we will constantly employ the principal means He has given us, namely, His Word. As Peter insisted, spiritually dead sinners can be born again by only one means: "the living and abiding Word of God" (1 Peter 1:23).

Third, Jesus said that the new birth is *revealed by its effects*: "The wind blows where it wishes, and you hear its sound, but you do not know where it comes from or where it goes. So it is with everyone who is born of the Spirit" (John 3:8). Those of us who have lived in Florida know about hurricanes. But we do not see the wind blowing; rather, we see the palms trees bending over and the debris flying. Likewise, we cannot see the new birth, but we observe its effects in our lives.

This poses a challenge for us today. The term *born again* has become popular. Surveys show that the majority of Americans consider themselves to be born again, by which they mean that they have had some spiritual experience. But for many, there has been no real change in their lives. When it comes to issues such as sexual sin, their conduct in marriage, their use of time and money, and their life ambitions, a great many so-called "born-again" people are no different than non-Christians. This is a problem because, according to the Bible, if we have not been changed, we have not been born again, regardless of any spiritual experiences we think we have had. To be born again, Paul said, is to be "created after the likeness of God in true righteousness and holiness" (Eph. 4:24). If our witness of the gospel is to be true and accurate, then we must present people with this reality.

Evidences of the New Birth

What, then, are evidences of the new birth? Spurgeon lists several, beginning with faith in Christ and in His gospel. Those who are born again have come to Jesus for their salvation, believe the Bible, and defend its doctrines. Also, there is repentance from sin: Spurgeon says, "Sorrow for sin is one of the sure signs of the new nature."[7] Those who are born again do not merely hate the misery that results from their sin, they despise their sin itself. Next is prayer. The first thing said about Paul after his rebirth was "Behold, he is praying" (Acts 9:11). Spurgeon sums up the effects of the new birth as the possession of a new life with new desires such as an interest in God, a love for His people, a joy in worship, and a hunger for God's Word.[8] This is what Ezekiel foretold—a rebirth that results in cleansing from sin and a new desire for holiness: "I will put my Spirit within you, and cause you to walk in my statutes" (Ezek. 36:27).

Sinclair Ferguson tells of a young man who came to church and eventually was converted. He told an elder: "I can't believe how much this church has changed within the last few weeks. The hymns are so lively now. The worship is so wonderfully meaningful. Why, even the preacher is better!"[9] Have you experienced something like that? Spurgeon asks, "Do you feel [that] . . . now you love God, now you seek to please him, now spiritual realities are realities to you, now the blood of Jesus is your only trust, now you desire to be made holy, even as God is holy? If there is such new life as that in you, however feeble it may be, though it is only like the life of a new-born child, you are born again, and you may rejoice in that blessed fact."[10]

Jesus' teaching that the new birth is revealed in its effects not only challenges us to examine ourselves for such evidences, it encourages us in our weakness and gives us hope about what the future holds for us. The Holy Spirit's work does not end with the new birth—having made us alive, He goes on to bring us more and more to life, working in us the life of God and molding our character into Christlikeness. The new birth is the beginning of a lifelong process of spiritual animation and growth, and is the pledge of glorious things yet to come. How wonderful that Christians are no longer what we once were, but how wonderful it also is that we someday will become what we are not yet. Paul says, "He who began a good work in you will bring it to completion at the day of Jesus Christ" (Phil. 1:6).

The New Birth Experienced

Ultimately, the new birth must not be explained but experienced. It does us no good to understand the new birth unless we have personally experienced it through a relationship with Jesus Christ.

One man who was truly born again is Tom Papania. His grandfather was one of the original mobsters who brought the Mafia to America from Sicily. His upbringing was savage, and at age 10 he vowed that he would never shed another tear. He grew up as a thief, an extortionist, and a murderer. His heart was so cold that even hardened criminals found it hard to look into his eyes, seeing nothing there but death.

However, God began to speak to Papania's heart. Though he tried not to listen, he felt convicted about his many evil deeds. But wanting to rob God of the chance to punish him with death, he put a gun to his head and was about to pull the trigger. Just then, the phone rang. It was a man he had met and who had been inviting him to church. Just to prove that God was wrong, he put down the gun and agreed to attend the man's church. When the service was over, the minister greeted him at the door. He said: "I have something I want to say to you, but I don't want to offend you. The eyes are the window of the soul. When you first came in here, I looked into your eyes, and all I could see was a little boy crying, wanting to be loved."

The pastor had exposed Papania's most painful secret, so the mobster went back that night to murder him. But to his amazement, he could not go through with it. Instead, he talked with the minister, who asked him whether he knew Jesus. He told Papania that he needed to be born again. The mobster just laughed. "Pastor," he said, "if these people in this church found out who I was, they'd throw both of us out of here. I'm probably the biggest sinner you'll ever see if you live to be a million years old. These people don't want me. I'm a sinner." He went on to recount his crimes, and before he knew it, he found himself kneeling on the ground, confessing his sins to God and opening the door of his heart to let Jesus in. He said, "I've found Jesus, and I've been searching for him all my life, and now that I have him, I'm not letting him go." Tom Papania went on to become a prison evangelist, his life changed by God's forgiveness and love in Jesus Christ. He was born again.[11]

Jesus says to us all: "You must be born again." You cannot cause yourself to be born again. But if God is calling you through His Word,

68

what you can do—and must do—is open your heart to Jesus in faith, receiving Him as your Lord and Savior. Through faith in Him, you will see and enter God's kingdom of salvation because you are born again. "Whoever believes in the Son has eternal life" (John 3:36a)—a life of love, truth, and holiness that will never end.

NOTES

1 Leon Morris, *The Gospel According to John*, revised (Grand Rapids, Mich.: Eerdmans Publishing, 1995), 188.

2 J. C. Ryle, *Expository Thoughts on the Gospels, John*, 3 vols. (London, England: James Clark, 1975), 1:122.

3 D. Martyn Lloyd-Jones, *Safe in the World* (Wheaton, Ill.: Crossway Books, 1988), 91.

4 Charles H. Spurgeon, *Metropolitan Tabernacle Pulpit*, 63 vols. (Pasadena, Texas: Pilgrim Publications, 1971), 25:57.

5 Morris, *The Gospel According to John*, 189.

6 Joseph "Skip" Ryan, *That You May Believe* (Wheaton, Ill.: Crossway Books, 2003), 100.

7 Spurgeon, *Metropolitan Tabernacle Pulpit*, 54:763.

8 Ibid., 54:764.

9 Cited from Ryan, *That You May Believe*, 106.

10 Spurgeon, *Metropolitan Tabernacle Pulpit*, 54:764.

11 Cited from Philip Graham Ryken, *Galatians* (Phillipsburg, N.J.: P&R Publishing, 2005), 35–36.

Questions for discussion and reflection:

1. Describe the setting in which Jesus encounters Nicodemus (John 3:1–21).

2. What type of man does Nicodemus represent? What sorts of things make it hard for a person like Nicodemus to have faith in Jesus? What about you and others you know?

3. In John 3:3, what does Jesus reveal to Nicodemus? Nicodemus claims to know many things. What is the right way to pursue knowledge of God?

4. What are some common but false views about the new birth?

5. Explain the three points Jesus teaches about the new birth. Can you find support for them elsewhere in Scripture?

6. How can we know that we are born again? What visible effects of the new birth can you see in your own life?

7. What is the relationship between the new birth and the cross? How is the new birth a product of God's love for us?

8. Imagine that a friend, co-worker, or neighbor comes to you uncertain of his or her salvation. How might you use the encounter between Jesus and Nicodemus to reassure this person or to call him or her to repentance and saving faith?

Chapter 6

THE ANSWER

John 3:9–21

Nicodemus said to him, "How can these things be?" Jesus answered him, "Are you the teacher of Israel and yet you do not understand these things?"   —*John 3:9–10*

I t is sometimes said that there is no such thing as a bad question. However, the Gospels show that this is not completely true, since Jesus frequently was approached by people with false questions intended to accuse or entrap Him. But whenever He received an honest question asked with a sincere desire for truth, Jesus always gave an honest answer. We also should give honest answers to honest questions in our witness to Christ.

An example is the question asked by Nicodemus in John 3:9. Jesus had confronted this Pharisee with his need to be born again. Nicodemus was puzzled, as non-Christians often are with the gospel, and asked, "How can these things be?" His question must have been sincere, because Jesus answered with some of the most beloved and instructive statements ever heard.

Mankind's Ignorance of Divine Truth

Nicodemus came to Jesus talking about what he knew. "We know that you are a teacher come from God," he began (John 3:2b). But Jesus cut him off, saying that "unless one is born again he cannot see the kingdom of God" (John 3:3b). Nicodemus really did not know as much as he thought he did, and he immediately displayed his ignorance: "How can a man be born when he is old?" he inquired (John 3:4a). Jesus answered by explaining that He was speaking of a spiritual rebirth, not a physical one.

This led to Nicodemus's second question: "How can these things be?" (John 3:9). Clearly he did not grasp Jesus' point in John 3:5–8, which was that no amount of questions would lead him into truth until he first had been brought to spiritual life. Before he could receive answers, Nicodemus needed to experience what Jesus was talking about. Jesus therefore replied: "Are you the teacher of Israel and yet you do not understand these things? Truly, truly, I say to you, we speak of what we know, and bear witness to what we have seen, but you do not receive our testimony. If I have told you earthly things and you do not believe, how can you believe if I tell you heavenly things?" (John 3:10–12).

The problem Nicodemus faced is the problem all of mankind faces: ignorance of divine and heavenly truth. This ignorance needs to be emphasized today, when mankind is more arrogantly deceived than ever about our ability to learn and know things. If we are going to progress in spiritual truth, Jesus says, we first must confess that on our own we are ignorant of God and of godly things, that what makes sense to us about spiritual realities is normally wrong, and that apart from God's gracious intervention we can only persist in ignorance and folly. This is a point that Christians should make in explaining the gospel.

Jesus presented two reasons why mankind is ignorant of divine truth. The first is that we have no access to the necessary information: "Truly, truly, I say to you, we speak of what we know, and bear witness to what we have seen" (John 3:11a). Jesus' use of "we" was probably a response to Nicodemus's statement in verse 2, "we know," and no doubt also referred to His fellow members of the Trinity—a rather more influential group than Nicodemus's. Jesus was saying: "You and your associates know about things you see in your world. What I and

My associates know is based on what We have seen in heaven." He then elaborated, saying, "No one has ascended into heaven except he who descended from heaven, the Son of Man" (John 3:13). His point was that unless someone had been in heaven, as He had, that person had no way of knowing heavenly things. Therefore, the wise thing was to listen to Jesus.

It is not that nothing can be known of God in this world. David wrote in Psalm 8 about looking up at the stars at night and seeing a display of God's majesty. But there are many vital matters about which we human beings simply cannot know by our own study or investigation. What does God require? How can one who has sinned be forgiven? What does the future hold for us? No matter how brilliant someone is or how much effort he applies, he cannot find answers to questions such as these on his own. This is why the entire history of philosophy is one of confusion and despair. Man lacks the information to answer the great questions of God and eternity. Job asked, "Can you find out the deep things of God?" (Job 11:7a). His answer was no! "It is higher than heaven—what can you do? Deeper than Sheol—what can you know?" (Job. 11: 8).

What man needs, therefore, is a Word from God. We need God to teach us. This is what the Bible provides: divine revelation. Not one of the biblical authors says, "Now here are some interesting things I have been thinking about." Not one says, "I have some ideas I want to share with you." They all say, "The Lord said to me . . ." or "This is the Word of the Lord. . . ." The Bible is revelation from God through human authors. Peter explains, "Men spoke from God as they were carried along by the Holy Spirit" (2 Peter 1:21). The Bible tells us what we need to know about divine things and the way of salvation. This is another point Christians should make when explaining the gospel from the Bible.

So a lack of information is the first of Nicodemus's and mankind's problems. The solution is God's teaching in the Bible. Of course, Nicodemus *had* the Bible, which was why Jesus asked how a teacher of Israel could be so ignorant. This points to a second problem, namely, that fallen mankind is not able to receive and understand God's teaching.

We find this truth demonstrated all through John's Gospel as men and women constantly misunderstood what Jesus said. For instance, Jesus offered the woman by the well a gift of "living water," and she thought He was talking about plumbing. Jesus fed the five thousand, then taught, "I am the bread of life," but His hearers asked how someone could eat His flesh. The people had His teaching but lacked the ability to grasp it.

The same was true of Nicodemus when it came to Jesus' teaching on the new birth. Jesus asked him, "Are you the teacher of Israel and yet you do not understand these things?" (John 3:10). This shows that the Scriptures are not enough without the regenerating work of the Spirit. Even with the Bible, we don't understand the things of God until the Spirit enables us to do so. Nicodemus was like so many brilliant and learned scholars today who know vast amounts of information about the Bible but cannot grasp its truth. Arthur W. Pink rightly warns: "The fact that a preacher has graduated with honors from some theological center is no proof that he is a man taught of the Holy Spirit. No dependence can be placed on human learning."[1] The reason is that no one can understand the Bible without the ministry of the Spirit.

The problem is not that the Bible is unclear or inherently difficult to understand. The problem, Jesus said, is that "you do not receive our testimony" (John 3:11b). This is why unregenerate people cannot understand God's Word: it is unacceptable to them. Being told that he needed to be born again offended Nicodemus's pride and cut against everything he had always believed. If that is true of earthly things, Jesus said in verse 12—and by "earthly things" He seems to have been referring to things that had earthly analogies, such as the new birth, which could be understood in terms of natural childbirth—how much more is it true of heavenly things, which are not so easily illustrated? Because of sin, people's hearts are hardened against the message of God's Word, and that is why they cannot grasp its truth (see Eph. 4:18).

I recently saw an article about a series of interviews with the singer Bono, of the rock band U2, that bore this out. Most interviewers hang on the words of rock stars and heap praise on all their thoughts. But this journalist asked Bono whether he agreed that religion is the cause of "appalling problems." Bono answered that it depends on the religion. He divided them between "Grace and Karma." Karma is the idea that what goes around comes around, that we ultimately end up getting what we deserve. In one form or another, this is what every religion apart from Christianity teaches. "I'd be in big trouble if Karma was going to finally be my judge," Bono said. "It doesn't excuse my mistakes, but I'm holding out for Grace. I'm holding out that Jesus took my sins onto the Cross. . . . It's not our own good works that get us through the gates of Heaven." That was a clear and humble presentation of the Christian gospel from the lips of one of the most popular people on the planet. So did the journalist praise Bono's message? Hardly. Even a rock star is rejected when he presents Jesus Christ. The interviewer replied, "The Son of God who takes away the sins of the world . . . it's close to lunacy, in my view."[2]

If people do not like to hear about the cross, they certainly do not like to be told they are ignorant. But this teaching is essential, as Jesus' example shows. Until people realize that the only way to know the truth is through God's Word and until they are humbled so as to see their need for the illuminating ministry of the Holy Spirit, they can never escape the darkness and find the light of Christ.

This reminds Christian evangelists once again of our responsibility to pray for unbelievers. Only God can enlighten the mind and open the heart to His gospel. So our witness of the gospel should be preceded by and followed with prayer. Apart from a willingness that comes only from God and the new spiritual life that only God can give, our witness will never lead to faith and salvation. But God often grants His grace in response to the prayers of His faithful evangelists.

The Source of the New Birth

Nicodemus was not born again and therefore was not able to understand. But his questions were sincere and, starting in verse 14, Jesus gave him a series of glorious answers. These answers should be included in our witness to unbelievers.

How can one be born again? Jesus' first answer was that the new birth is possible because of the *sacrifice of the Son of Man*. This is the *cause* of the new birth.

"Son of Man" is the title Jesus used most frequently for Himself. Most people think "Son of Man" is a reference to Jesus' humanity. But there is more to it than that. The term comes from a vision shown to Daniel, in which he was given the privilege of looking into heaven, much as John would do in writing the book of Revelation. Daniel saw "the Ancient of Days"—a reference to God the Father—taking His heavenly throne. Then he saw that "with the clouds of heaven there came one like a son of man, and he came to the Ancient of Days and was presented before him. And to him was given dominion and glory and a kingdom" (Dan. 7:9–14a). What Daniel saw was the ascension of Jesus into heaven. "Son of Man," therefore, is a title for the glorious Prince of heaven who humbled Himself to come to the earth and take on a human form, and having accomplished the work of our salvation, ascended to heaven in a cloud of glory to receive His kingdom from the Father.

Jesus used this term here for the first time in John's Gospel. The new birth is made possible, He said, by the sacrifice of the Son of Man. He made this point with an example from the Scriptures: "As Moses lifted up the serpent in the wilderness, so must the Son of Man be lifted up" (John 3:14). These words recall an event from the time of Moses. The Israelites spoke in rebellion against God, so He sent fiery serpents among them as punishment. The snakes bit the people and caused many to die (Num. 21:4–6). Realizing they had sinned, the people asked Moses to intercede with God. When Moses did, God gave him an instructive remedy. He told Moses to make a snake of bronze and set it on a pole. When someone was bitten, he or she was to look to the bronze snake; those who did so would live (Num. 21:8).

According to Jesus, this event symbolized His mission to remedy our need. Like the Israelites, we have sinned, and the punishment for sin is the curse of death. We, too, have been bitten by the Serpent and received his deadly poison. But Jesus entered the world to be lifted up on the cross and bear the curse our sins deserve. The way of salvation, then, is not by self-improvement or human striving. Salvation is by looking to the crucified Christ in faith to be forgiven and live.

There are two "musts" in John 3. Jesus said, "You *must* be born again" (John 3:7, emphasis added). But He added, "As Moses lifted up the serpent . . . so *must* the Son of Man be lifted up" (John 3:14, emphasis added). These two "musts" go together. Christ died for our sins so that "whoever believes in him may have eternal life" (John 3:15).

This, then, is the first answer to Nicodemus's question, "How can these things be?" Because Jesus died for us, the Holy Spirit comes to make us born again. Through faith in the Son of Man lifted up, sinners gain eternal life.

Jesus' next answer to Nicodemus comes in John 3:16. Having named *the Son's sacrifice* as the *cause* of the new birth, Jesus gave *the love of the Father* as the *reason* for the new birth: "For God so loved the world, that he gave his only Son, that whoever believes in him should not perish but have eternal life." How simple, profound, and wonderful this is. The reason we can be born again, receiving eternal life, is that God loves the world.

Ours is not a very good world. The Bible shows that as soon as sin entered the world, people began hating, fighting, and killing one another. Everything in this world dies, and multitudes suffer all the time. Philosophers despair because there is no hope within this world.

Some people blame God for tyranny, injustice, and suffering, but the truth is that we are to blame. God has condemned the world because of its sin. In Noah's time, "The LORD saw that the wickedness of man was great in the earth, and that every intention of the thoughts of his heart was only evil continually" (Gen. 6:5). Mankind has not gotten better since then, and God still looks at the world and sees great and continual evil.

Some people think they are different. But I ask you, would you be willing for a transcript to be made of all your thoughts, from the time you got up this morning until now, and for that transcript to be read before your church? How much worse would it be for our thoughts to be read before God! But they are. Psalm 139 says, "O LORD, you have searched me and known me! . . . You discern my thoughts from afar . . . and are acquainted with all my ways" (vv. 1–3).

So how can we be saved? How can we be born again? The answer is that we can be saved because the Father loves us and sent His Son to die for our sins. Some people think that God accepts us only because Jesus forces Him to. But it was a loving Father who sent His Son.

God's glorious love is not like the love we know in this world. We love only when something is lovely or lovable. James Dobson tells a story of his beautiful daughter as a little girl. Everyone loved her and showered her with affection. But then she had an accident and her face was swollen and ugly for several weeks. During that time, people treated her with contempt. That is how our world loves! But God loves the unloved and the unlovely. God loves this world.

People say, "Why doesn't God do something about this world?" But He has! He has given the new birth so that we might enter eternal life, and He did it by sending His own Son to die for us on the cross. "The measure of love is how much it gives," says J. I. Packer, and "the measure of the love of God is the gift of His only Son to be made man, and to die for sins, and so to become the one mediator who can bring us to God. No wonder Paul speaks of God's love as 'great' and passing knowledge! (Eph. 2:4)."[3]

This means there is hope for this world and hope for you. You can have a new start. Why? Because God so loved. You can have a new life. How? By receiving God's love through faith in Christ. Is there any message more wonderful or more urgent than this: "God so loved the world, that he gave his only Son, that whoever believes in him should not perish but have eternal life" (John 3:16)?

Jesus' first answer to Nicodemus was the sacrifice of the Son and His second was the love of the Father, so we would expect His third answer to deal with the Holy Spirit. This is right. Jesus said, "This is the judgment: the light has come into the world, and people loved the darkness rather than the light because their deeds were evil. . . . But whoever does what is true comes to the light" (John 3:19–21a). When Jesus was in the world, He was the light. Now, the Holy Spirit shines the light of Christ through God's Word. This, then, is the third answer to Nicodemus's question, "How can these things be?" How is it that you can be born again? Because the light of Christ is shining today through *the illuminating work of God's Spirit.* This is the *means* of the new birth; this is how people are born again today.

Peter wrote, "You have been born again, not of perishable seed but of imperishable, through the living and abiding word of God" (1 Peter 1:23). Christ's light shines through the Word of God—as it is read, preached, and witnessed—and people are born again because the Holy Spirit shines that Word in their hearts. "The Spirit of truth . . . will guide you into all the truth," Jesus said. "He will glorify me, for he will take what is mine and declare it to you" (John 16:13–14).

Nicodemus was right that Jesus' teaching on the new birth was stupendous. He asked, "How can this be?" It was a very good question. Jesus answered with very good news. There is life through His death, there is love from the heart of God, and there is light shining in God's Word through the Holy Spirit. This is why we can be born again.

In the Face of Christ

We began by considering Nicodemus's ignorance of divine things. Like everyone else, he needed a word from God. According to John, the truest Word ever revealed from God is Jesus Christ Himself. "In the beginning was the Word," John began. "In him was life, and the life was the light of men" (John 1:1, 4). Nicodemus had questions; Jesus not only had answers, but is Himself the Answer. To be born again, as Paul said, is to see "the light of the knowledge of the glory of God in the face of Jesus Christ" (2 Cor. 4:6).

Nicodemus asked, "How can these things be?" In other words, he asked, "How can I be born again?" Have you asked that question? Nothing else in life matters compared to this! The answers Jesus gave are that the Son of Man was lifted up so that sinners who believe can have eternal life; that the eternal Father has loved the world, and so He sent His only Son, promising that anyone who believes in Him will have eternal life; and that through God's Word, the Holy Spirit shines still today, so that we can turn from our evil deeds to walk in the light of Christ. Those answers are true. But they mean nothing unless you come to Jesus Himself. They mean nothing for others unless they, too, come to Jesus. Ultimately, to be born again is to receive Jesus and give yourself to Him in return. Only those who believe on Him are born again into eternal life.

So what happened to Nicodemus? This encounter ends without any definite conclusion. But Nicodemus shows up again in John 7, speaking up for Jesus in the Sanhedrin. The Spirit was still working on his heart and he had not forgotten his nighttime meeting. Finally, the day came when what Jesus foretold that night happened, and Nicodemus was there. He must have recalled Jesus' words as he watched Him dying on the cross: "The Son of Man [must] be lifted up, that whoever believes in him may have eternal life" (John 3:14b–15). Finally, then, Nicodemus saw the light. He saw not merely a teacher, not simply a rabbi, and not just a worker of miracles. He saw upon that cross the Savior of his soul. He saw his sins washed clean by the precious blood of Christ. He was born again.

How do we know? We know because of what happened next. John says: "Joseph of Arimathea, who was a disciple of Jesus, but secretly for fear of the Jews, asked Pilate that he might take away the body of Jesus, and Pilate gave him permission. So he came and took away his body. Nicodemus also, who earlier had come to Jesus by night, came" (John 19:38–39a). Finally, Nicodemus came out to Jesus in the light of day, publicly identifying himself with Christ, come what may. "So it is," Jesus had said, "with everyone who is born of the Spirit" (John 3:8b).

What an exciting ending to Nicodemus's story! But it had not yet happened when Jesus was explaining the new birth. Nicodemus reminds us again that our witness is never wasted. His example also reminds us of the need for us to follow up with those who have heard the gospel. Understanding their challenges and trials, we should remember them in prayer before the Lord. As we have opportunities, we should inquire about their souls and encourage them in seeking the truth about Jesus. In many instances, and often in surprising ways, God reveals Himself finally and opens eyes to His light. Let us never underestimate how powerful are the seeds of the gospel, and let us marvel at the saving grace of God when each sinner repents, believes, and finds salvation at the cross of our Savior.

NOTES

---

[1] Arthur W. Pink, *Exposition of the Gospel of John* (Grand Rapids, Mich.: Zondervan, 1975), 124.

[2] Gene Edward Veith, "Salty Dogma," *WORLD*, Aug. 4, 2005.

[3] J. I. Packer, *Knowing God* (Downers Grove, Ill.: InterVarsity Press, 1974), 114.

Questions for discussion and reflection:

1. What honest questions do people today have about Christianity and the Bible that we should be prepared to answer?

2. The chapter presents two reasons why people are ignorant of divine truth. Have you encountered this ignorance in your interactions with people? How can you shape your witness to help them? What does this issue suggest about the importance of prayer in our witnessing?

3. Have you ever met someone who thought the message of the gospel was "lunacy"? How did you respond? How should we handle the fact that many people simply dislike the gospel?

4. As Moses told the Israelites to look to the bronze serpent, the Bible tells us to "look to Jesus" for our salvation. What does it mean to look to Jesus? How can we be sure that our understanding of Jesus is the biblical one? Are there certain truths we must believe in order to be saved? What are they?

5. Why does the author say the cross of Jesus Christ is the *cause* of the new birth? How should this reality influence our approach to sharing the gospel?

6. What is the role of the Holy Spirit in bringing us to faith? How does the Spirit "illuminate" the Bible? How have you experienced this? Does this mean that each of us can have a private interpretation of what the Bible means? If not, why not?

7. Nicodemus' conversion seems to have come about through a lengthy process. How does this compare with your own conversion or that of other Christians you know? How should the example of Nicodemus influence your approach to evangelism?

8. Can you identify at least one person who has clearly heard the gospel but has not yet believed? Pray for that person.

Chapter 7

THE GOSPEL OF LOVE

John 3:16

"For God so loved the world, that he gave his only Son, that whoever believes in him should not perish but have eternal life."   —*John 3:16*

Because so many Americans watch sports events, some Christians attempt to present a gospel witness in stadiums and arenas. Perhaps you have seen the signs, held up in the crowd or posted on a wall. Most commonly, the signs have this short message: "JN 3:16." The idea is that people will know or find out that "JN" is shorthand for the Gospel of John and that "3:16" means chapter 3, verse 16. The hope is that great things will happen if people will merely pick up a Bible and read this one verse: "For God so loved the world, that he gave his only Son, that whoever believes in him should not perish but have eternal life."

John 3:16 is a verse beloved by evangelists because it answers an essential question, namely, "What is the gospel?" This is not a trivial matter. The fact is that the witness of many Christians is greatly hampered by confusion over the content of the Christian gospel. To some, the gospel is simply an invitation for a person to allow God to come into his or her heart. But what does this mean? Is this what God offers the world? Given this kind of confusion, it is essential for those who witness the gospel to know what the gospel is. John 3:16 answers with a simple statement of God's love for us in Jesus Christ. Bruce Milne describes the verse as "a masterly and moving summary of the gospel, cast in terms of the love of God."[1]

God's Amazing Love

John 3:16 presents us with the Bible's greatest theme: God's love for us through Jesus Christ. This is a message that the world needs to hear and that our witness must proclaim. Therefore, a brief study of God's love as depicted in the Bible is sure to be helpful. What can Christians say about God's love?

The apostle Paul writes that God's love is *great*: "God, being rich in mercy, because of the *great love* with which he loved us, even when we were dead in our trespasses, made us alive together with Christ" (Eph. 2:4–5a, emphasis added). We tend to overuse the word *great*. For instance, we say we had a "great time" if we enjoyed ourselves at all. Or if God blesses us a bit in ministry, we say we had a "great success." Overused like this, the word *great* loses some of its force. But when the Bible says God's love is great, it means it! God's love for the world was great in the amazing care He exercised in creating it; nature reveals the most loving craftsmanship. But how much greater is the love of God that was revealed in the gift of His Son. The Greek word Paul uses for "great" (*pollein*) is used to describe an overflowing harvest or intense emotions. God's love truly deserves to be called great.

Paul elsewhere describes God's love as *unfathomable*. In his letter to the Ephesians, he prays that believers "may have strength to comprehend with all the saints what is the breadth and length and height and depth, and to know the love of Christ that surpasses knowledge" (Eph. 3:18–19a). What we are to comprehend about the dimensions of God's love is that they are beyond measure. It is possible to exhaust the love of a spouse or of friends—and in extreme cases, even of siblings or parents. But it is not possible to exhaust the love of God. In his great hymn titled "The Love of God," Frederick M. Lehman wrote:

84

The love of God is greater far than tongue or pen can ever tell,
It goes beyond the highest star, and reaches to the lowest hell.

God's love also can be described in terms of all His other attributes. The attributes of God are aspects of His character or being; to list them is to describe what God is like. However, many make the great mistake of pitting one of God's attributes against another. Many of us, for instance, prefer God's love to His holiness. But we must never think that we must or can choose between the two. God's holiness is a loving holiness and His love is a holy love. Our generation has spoiled much of the idea of love—particularly romantic love—by joining it with sin. But God does not and cannot do that. His love is joined to holy purposes, and His love for us will have the ultimate result of bringing us to a gloriously holy condition. When I am counseling a couple prior to their wedding, I often hear one of them (usually the bride) say, "I never want to change him!" I always pause, lean forward, look her in the eye, and say: "You will! You will!" God's love never says, "I don't want to change you." Because God's love is holy, He intends to change us by loving means, so that we will become the holy people we were always meant to be.

God is almighty, and therefore His is an almighty love. This means He is able to do all that His love desires for us. J. I. Packer writes that God's love "has at its heart an almighty purpose to bless which cannot be thwarted."[2] Paul rightly asks who shall separate us from this love. "I am sure," he answers, "that neither death nor life, nor angels nor rulers, nor things present nor things to come, nor powers, nor height nor depth, nor anything else in all creation, will be able to separate us from the love of God in Christ Jesus our Lord" (Rom. 8:38–39).

Moreover, as God is unchangeable, so His love is unchangeable. John Owen writes: "Though we change every day, yet his love does not change. If anything in us or on our part could stop God loving us, then he long ago would have turned away from us. It is because his love is fixed and unchangeable that the Father shows us infinite patience and forbearance. If his love was not unchangeable, we would perish."[3]

God is eternal, and so is His love. Paul says, "He chose us in [Christ] before the foundation of the world" (Eph. 1:4). God's love for us originated in eternity past, and it flows to eternity future. God says, "I have loved you with an everlasting love" (Jer. 31:3). He adds, "For the mountains may depart and the hills be removed, but my steadfast love shall not depart from you" (Isa. 54:10a).

Moreover, as God is sovereign, so is His love. Ephesians 1:5–6a says, "In love he predestined us for adoption through Jesus Christ, according to the purpose of his will, to the praise of his glorious grace." James Montgomery Boice writes: "God's love is a sovereign one . . . his love is uninfluenced by anything in the creature. And if that is so, it is the same as saying that the cause of God's love lies only in himself. . . . In Scripture no cause for God's love other than his electing will is ever given."[4] This was God's explanation to the Israelites for the love He showed them in the exodus: "It was not because you were more in number than any other people that the Lord set his love on you and chose you, for you were the fewest of all peoples, but it is because the Lord loves you" (Deut. 7:7–8a).

Lastly, we should note that God is infinite, and so is His love. There is no greater proof of this than John's statement that God loved "the world." There is an infinite distance between God and this wicked world. God tells us, "As the heavens are higher than the earth, so are my ways higher than your ways and my thoughts than your thoughts" (Isa. 55:9). Our world has rebelled against God, flouting His authority and mocking His ways. Because of this, most people reject God's rule over their lives. Paul says, "Although they knew God, they did not honor him as God or give thanks to him, but they became futile in their thinking, and their foolish hearts were darkened" (Rom. 1:21). That is an accurate description of our world today. The distance between us and God is infinite in every way. But God's love is infinitely great to span that distance.

When John speaks of "the world," he is being intentionally provocative. Old Testament Jews believed that God loved them, but rejected the idea that God loved anyone else. Leon Morris explains: "It is a distinctively Christian idea that God's love is wide enough to embrace all people. His love is not confined to any national group or spiritual elite."[5] The same is true today. John does not say that God sent Jesus because He loved religious people or Christians, but because "God so loved the world." This is why the message of Jesus Christ is good news for everyone. Romans 5:8 tells us, "God shows his love for us in that while we were still sinners, Christ died for us."

God's Giving Love

This brings us to the particular point that John 3:16 stresses: God's love is a *giving* love. The Greek language has four words that can be translated as "love," each pointing to a different kind of love. The first is *storge*, which is family love. Whatever they think of each other, family members are to be loyal. The second is *eros*, which is romantic or sexual love. The third word is *philos*, which is the love of friendship or attraction. The word *philosophy* means a love of wisdom. This is a receiving love; it is based on what we get and how good something or someone makes us feel. But the New Testament stresses a fourth kind of love, using the Greek word *agape*. This is giving love. It is not based on what we receive but on what we give. Agape love has its classic definition in John 3:16: "For God so loved the world, that he gave his only Son."

The greatness of God's love for the world is seen most clearly in the gift that He gave: "his only Son." John says not merely that God loved the world, but that "God *so* loved the world." The word *so* indicates both the manner in which God loved the world—by giving His Son—and the strength of God's love for the world. How do we measure God's love for us? By calculating the infinite value of His precious Son, Jesus Christ.

John refers to Jesus as God's "only Son." We are undoubtedly intended to reflect upon this in light of our love for our own children. Even though we are corrupted by sin, it is natural for us to love our children with great intensity. Mothers exhaust themselves rocking babies to sleep. Fathers spend long hours fixing bikes and playing games in which they would have no interest were it not for their children. Parents weary themselves with extra jobs to clothe, feed, and educate their children. To neglect our children, as many do today, is so obviously wrong that it is broadly condemned. Nature knows no greater love than that of a parent for his or her child, and Christ is God the Father's only child. The Father many times spoke of His love for His Son, and Jesus often basked in His Father's love. So in giving His only Son, God truly was giving His very heart. The Puritan John Flavel asks: "Who would part with a son for the sake of his dearest friends? But God gave him to, and delivered him for enemies: O love unspeakable!"[6] God could not possibly love this world more or better than He did in giving His beloved only Son.

In saying that God gave His only Son, John 3:16 corrects a terrible but common mistake in the way people think about God the Father. Because Jesus died to satisfy God's justice, some think that God's love is caused by Christ's sacrifice, and even that the Father's love is reluctant or half-hearted. But John 3:16 teaches exactly the opposite. J. C. Ryle notes: "The gift of Christ . . . is the result of God's love to the world, and not the cause. To say that God loves us because Christ died for us, is wretched theology indeed. But to say that Christ came into the world in consequence of the love of God, is scriptural truth."[7] God loved this evil world not after but before the Savior came to turn our hearts back to heaven; God's love is the reason we can be forgiven and born again to inherit eternal life.

When John says that God "gave" His only Son, what exactly does he mean? According to the Bible, the Father sent the eternal and glorious Son into this world to take up our mortal nature, with all the weakness and suffering that involved, yet without sin (see Heb. 2:17). Jesus states thirty-nine times in John's Gospel that the Father "sent" Him into the world on a mission of salvation. God sent Him to reveal His truth, to proclaim the good news of salvation, and especially to do the work needed for the salvation of those who believe. Ryle says: "Christ is God the Father's gift to a lost and sinful world. He was given generally to be the Saviour, the Redeemer, the Friend of sinners,—to make an atonement sufficient for all,—and to provide a redemption large enough for all. To effect this, the Father freely gave Him up to be despised, rejected, mocked, crucified, and counted guilty and accursed for our sakes."[8]

This means that when we read that God "gave his only Son," we should think of the cross where Jesus suffered and died that we might be forgiven of our sins. So great is His love that if our redemption from sin required the tortuous death of His only Son—even the outpouring of His own wrath upon His most beloved child—God was willing to give Him for this. Jeremiah Burroughs marvels:

> Behold the infinite love of God to mankind and the love of Jesus Christ that, rather than God see the children of men to perish eternally, He would send His Son to take our nature upon Him and thus suffer such dreadful things. Herein God shows His love. . . . It pleased the Father to break His Son and to pour out His blood. Here is the love of God and of Jesus Christ. Oh, what a powerful, mighty, drawing, efficacious meditation this should be to us![9]

During the darkest times of World War I, a conflict that took the lives of a shocking number of English sons, a man took his little boy out for a walk at night. The boy noticed that some of the houses had stars in the windows. "That comes from this terrible war, laddie," the father explained. "It shows that these people have given a son." They walked a bit further, then the young boy stopped and pointed to the sky, where a bright evening star had appeared. He said, "Daddy, God must have given a Son, too." Morris remarks: "That is it. In the terrible war against evil, God gave his Son. That is the way evil was defeated. God paid the price."[10]

God's gift, therefore, was not only infinite in value, it was perfectly suited to our greatest need. John 3:16 says, "For God so loved the world, that he gave his only Son, that whoever believes in him should not perish but have eternal life." We might prefer that God had done something other than send His only Son to be our Savior. But God's love addressed our true and greatest need. This is why, whenever the New Testament speaks of God's love, it almost invariably does so in terms of the atoning work of Christ upon the cross. John 3:16 is a typical example. In the previous two verses, Jesus told Nicodemus, "As Moses lifted up the serpent in the wilderness, so must the Son of Man be lifted up, that whoever believes in him may have eternal life" (John 3:14–15). That was an allusion to His death on the cross. This, then, is how the world knows and receives God's love. It is not because we are able to love one another a bit or because there is beauty in the world; rather, it is because God sent Jesus to die for our sins. John writes in his first epistle, "In this the love of God was made manifest among us, that God sent his only Son into the world. . . . He loved us and sent his Son to be the propitiation for our sins" (1 John 4:9–10).

Receiving God's Love

Flavel, the Puritan, concludes his study of John 3:16 with three keen observations. First, he says, this verse shows us "The exceeding preciousness of souls, and at what a high rate God values them, that he will give his Son, his only Son out of his bosom, as a ransom for them."[11] Surely this argues that we ought to labor with all our might to bring people to salvation. We should tell them how precious their souls are to God, and what God has done for their salvation. John 3:16 says that "whoever believes should not perish but have eternal life." It is through our witness that they can believe. It is because we take an interest in their souls, because we speak earnestly to them about Jesus, and because we invite them to join us at church and hear God's Word that souls are saved today.

This task must apply most urgently to our own children. It is dismaying to see how little interest so many parents take in the souls of their children. Since we love them, and since their souls are so precious to

God, we should be especially determined to set them a godly example, pray with and for them, teach them God's Word, and involve them in the worship and life of the church.

Second, Flavel notes, since God has given us His Son, we may be confident of receiving every other help and mercy we need to endure this life and arrive safely in heaven. This confidence should give us peace in every storm and trust in the face of life's trials.

This point reminds us that the gospel proclaims more than the receipt of a ticket to heaven when we die. The gospel also proclaims God's loving care in this present life. What a message this is for the hurting world around us. And it should change our own attitudes in a mighty way. Knowing how much God has already given us—His very best in the person of His Son—we should trust His love and come to Him with a holy boldness in prayer. Paul reasoned, "He who did not spare his own Son but gave him up for us all, how will he not also with him graciously give us all things?" (Rom. 8:32). God will not withhold anything we need, having already given His Son Jesus, so we should not shrink from asking for and confidently awaiting anything we truly need.

In an earlier chapter, I recounted my witness to a group of Muslims in the African country of Uganda. One of their chief complaints was that God had not been answering their prayers. They were poor, hungry, and oppressed, and God was not helping. So I asked them, "When you pray to God, what name do you give Him?" They replied, "Allah." I replied: "That is why God does not answer your prayers. But when you pray to Him in the name of Jesus, His own Son, then God will receive you as His own beloved children." I then cited John 1:12: "To all who did receive [Jesus], who believed in his name, he gave the right to become children of God." It was mainly this desire—a right desire—to know God's fatherly care that opened their hearts to the Lord. Many others who sorrow and grieve in this world will be led to Jesus by the relationship He provides us as children of the heavenly Father.

Third, Flavel says, "If the greatest love hath been manifested in giving Christ to the world, then it follows that the greatest evil and wickedness is manifested in despising, slighting, and rejecting Christ."[12] There can be no greater condemnation than to disregard the amazing love of God in giving His only Son to suffer in our place. What does God ask and expect of us? God demands what love always desires: to be received. Jesus said in John 6:29, "This is the work of God, that you believe in him whom he has sent." John 3:16 says that God calls us to believe on Jesus Christ—to receive His love-gift through personal faith in Jesus. If we believe, He promises us "eternal life." But if we are so hardened of heart to refuse this matchless gift from God, the result is that we will "perish." Having spurned God's love on the cross, we must receive the just penalty for all our sins and especially for the chief sin of rejecting God's only Son. As the writer of Hebrews warns us, "How shall we escape if we neglect such a great salvation?" (Heb. 2:3). The Christian witness should press this reality upon the hearts of those who are reluctant to receive God's gift of His Son.

A Call to Love

There is one last application for those who believe in Christ and who are thus born again into eternal life. If God loved us by giving us His Son, we ought to love Him with all that we have in return.

Shortly after the end of the American Civil War, a man in farm clothes was seen kneeling at a gravestone in the soldiers' cemetery in Nashville, Tennessee. An observer came up and asked, "Is that the grave of your son?" The farmer replied, "No, I have seven children, all of them young, and a wife on my poor farm in Illinois. I was drafted and, despite the great hardship it would cause, I was required to join the Army. But on the morning I was to depart, this man, my neighbor's older son, came over and offered to take my place in the war." The observer solemnly asked, "What is that you are writing on his grave?" The farmer replied, "I am writing, 'He died for me.'"

With that same devotion, we should love God for His love in giving Jesus Christ to die for us. And we should express that devotion by loving others with the same kind of love God has shown to us. We are to show a love the world does not know—a love not based on getting, but a love that says, "God has given to me, so I want to love Him by giving to others." This giving love should beautify our marriages, enliven our friendships, glorify God in the church, and inspire in us a loving fervor in evangelism. This was John's own application in his first epistle, having spoken first of God's love for us in the giving of His Son: "Beloved, if God so loved us, we also ought to love one another" (1 John 4:11).

Living out God's amazing, giving love will be our strongest testimony to a loveless world. If we will only do so, others will learn of God's great love from us and will come to understand that by believing in Him, they, too, will have eternal life.

NOTES

[1] Bruce Milne, *The Message of John: Here Is Your King!* (Downers Grove, Ill.: InterVarsity Press, 1993), 77.

[2] J. I. Packer, *Knowing God* (Downers Grove, Ill.: InterVarsity Press, 1974), 250.

[3] John Owen, *Communion with God* (Edinburgh, Scotland, and Carlisle, Pa.: Banner of Truth Trust, 1991), 29–30.

[4] James Montgomery Boice, *Foundations of the Christian Faith* (Downers Grove, Ill.: InterVarsity Press, 1986), 337.

[5] Leon Morris, *The Gospel According to John*, revised (Grand Rapids, Mich.: Eerdmans Publishing, 1995), 203.

[6] John Flavel, *The Works of John Flavel*, 6 vols. (Edinburgh, Scotland, and Carlisle, Pa.: Banner of Truth Trust, 1820, reprint 1968), 1:68.

[7] J. C. Ryle, *Expository Thoughts on the Gospels: John*, 3 vols. (Edinburgh, Scotland, and Carlisle, Pa.: Banner of Truth Trust, 1999), 1:160.

[8] Ibid.

[9] Jeremiah Burroughs, *Gospel Worship* (Morgan, Penn.: Soli Deo Gloria, 1648, reprint 1990), 353.

[10] Leon Morris, *Reflections on the Gospel of John* (Peabody, Mass.: Hendrickson Publishers, 1986), 100.

[11] Flavel, *The Works of John Flavel*, 1:68.

[12] Ibid., 1:70.

Questions for discussion and reflection:

1. How is God's love different from human love? Review the list of God's attributes in this chapter. What difference does it make that they all are joined to the love of God?

2. To whom is God's love available today?

3. We tend to romanticize love or think of it as a feeling. But in the Bible, love is portrayed mainly as an act. In our spiritual lives, should we rely on feelings or on facts? How are the two different? How do they sometimes work together?

4. If someone were to ask you how you know God loves you, what evidence would you give?

5. When the Bible says that God "gave His only Son," what does it mean? According to the quotes from J. C. Ryle and Jeremiah Burroughs, what specifically did the Father give His Son to be and to do? How was God's gift of love perfectly suited to our greatest need?

6. How should the fact that God "so loved the world" inspire our dedication to sharing the gospel with other people? What does the fact that God gave His own Son to die for our sins say about His willingness to meet all our other needs?

Chapter 8

THE GOSPEL OF FAITH

John 3:16–18

"For God so loved the world, that he gave his only Son, that whoever believes in him should not perish but have eternal life." —*John 3:16*

My wife and I are blessed with five children, all of whom are still young. The various stages of their childhoods can be noted in terms of the treasures they cherish. Our oldest child, age 10, treasures her friends very dearly. Our oldest son, age 9, undoubtedly counts his baseball glove as chief among his possessions. Our 6-year-old treasures his favorite toys, and our two little girls, ages 4 and 2, still yearn for their "blankies" above all other things.

These children are treasures to their parents, and for this reason our great desire is that each of them would come to know something far greater as his or her chief material possession in life. It is a treasure that should be precious to young and old, for possession of it gains for us eternal life. It is God's gift that meets our greatest need and provides the greatest blessings we can ever imagine.

Our Greatest Possession: "Whoever Believes in Him"

John 3:16 is well-beloved because of what it tells us about God and His love. But this verse is also very instructive about this greatest of all possessions—faith. The Christian witness is an appeal for faith, both in the loving God who gave His Son and in Jesus Christ, the Savior who gives eternal life. Because of this, Christians need to be able to explain just what faith is. This is an important question that is bound to come up in conversations about the gospel. What, then, is saving faith?

The Bible's teaching on faith has been said to include three elements, each of which is known by a Latin name. First is *notitia,* or "knowledge." There are truths that a person must know in order to have faith. In other words, the Christian faith has content; it is not merely a spiritual feeling or experience. There are certain facts about God, Jesus Christ, and mankind that we must know and understand. This truth rules out any ideas of implicit or indirect faith. Biblical faith is far different from the "faith" of a man who, when asked what he believed, answered, "I believe what the church believes." When asked what the church believed, he said, "The church believes what I believe." Finally, when asked what he and the church believed, he replied, "We believe the same thing!" Such "faith," lacking personal knowledge, does not save.

The second element goes by the Latin word *assensus,* which means "assent." R. C. Sproul explains: "Intellectual assent involves the assurance or conviction that a certain proposition is true. When we say we believe George Washington was the first president of the United States, we mean that we affirm the truth of that proposition."[1]

At the heart of the Christian faith are beliefs about Jesus Christ. People may call themselves Christians but say, "I just don't believe Jesus was God, that He died for our sins, or that He was raised from the dead." They are not Christians, because these beliefs are necessary to saving faith. John concludes his Gospel by writing, "These [accounts of Jesus' ministry] are written so that you may believe that Jesus is the Christ, the Son of God, and that by believing you may have life in his name" (John 20:31). This verse shows the value of creedal statements such as the Apostles' Creed, which recount many truths that Christians must know *and* affirm, the most crucial of which are the facts of Jesus' life, death, and resurrection for our salvation.

There is a third element of saving faith. The Latin word *fiducia* signifies "trust" or "commitment." This element reminds us that it is not enough merely to affirm that certain statements are true. We also must embrace them personally, committing ourselves to what they mean. Ultimately, this final element of faith takes us beyond truth claims to a person. We must commit to Jesus Christ Himself, trusting in what He has done for us. Leon Morris describes it well: "Christian faith means the abandonment of trust in one's own achievements and a coming to rely on what Christ has done to bring us salvation."[2] James Montgomery Boice adds: "We turn from trusting in ourselves and instead trust God fully. We see the infinite worth and love of the Son of God, who gave himself for our salvation, and commit ourselves to him."[3]

There is an unfortunate tendency when it comes to interpreting John 3:16. John says, "whoever believes in him" will not perish. Some people think that "believing in" Jesus means nothing more than giving assent. They hang their hopes for heaven on this slender reed: "Sure, I believe in Jesus." They mean that they believe that He exists and agree with at least some of what the Bible says about Him. But the biblical teaching about Jesus means practically nothing to them. They "believe in" Jesus in much the same way a child "believes in" Santa Claus. It is the particular legend or story with which they were brought up.

But John means much more than this when he writes that whoever "believes in" Jesus Christ will not perish. In his outstanding study of John's Gospel, C. H. Dodd points out that this Greek construction translates a common Hebrew phrase in the Old Testament that employs a form of *amen*, a word that signifies something that is firmly held or established. Isaiah used it in his famous statement to King Ahaz: "If you are not firm in faith, you will not be firm at all" (Isa. 7:9b). Therefore, when John says "whoever believes in him," he is speaking of those who give their "Amen" to Jesus, embracing Him as a trustworthy Savior and committing themselves to Him.[4]

Perhaps the best illustration of saving faith is marriage. A couple is married through a wedding ceremony, in which vows are made. On the basis of these promises, a man and woman open their lives to each other, share all of their property, and give of themselves wholly. But what is the basis for all this? They do it because they trust each other to fulfill the vows they have made. This is very much what happens when someone believes on Jesus Christ, trusting His promises to be true and committing himself or herself to be His disciple.

At the beginning of this chapter of John's Gospel, Jesus described faith as "seeing": "Truly, truly, I say to you, unless one is born again he cannot see the kingdom of God" (John 3:3). Faith is having our eyes open so that we see Jesus for who He is. Until we are born again, we cannot and do not believe, because our sinful nature is opposed to faith. Therefore, to realize that you believe in Christ—that you accept what the Bible teaches, trust it as saving truth, and have personally committed yourself to Jesus—is to receive wonderfully good news. It means that you have been born again, since Jesus says that without the new birth you cannot even see, much less enter, God's kingdom.

Skip Ryan learned this from a woman he calls "the Ladybug." The wife of a philosophy professor at the local university, she came to his church every week to scowl at him while he preached. She drove an old Volkswagen "bug" that she had painted red with black spots, just like her namesake insect. Week after week she attended his preaching. But one Sunday, he noticed her posture changing—she melted into a different person right before his eyes. When he approached her afterward, she explained what had happened: "The light has come on. I understand. The Lord has worked in my heart." In short, she had been born again. A couple of days later, she came into his office to talk about it, and there she revealed a better grasp of doctrine than Ryan had. He asked, "What happened to you the other day when you decided to follow Jesus?" She replied: "Young man, the only thing I had decided to do was how I was going to run you over in my Volkswagen. *Jesus* decided that I was going to be His follower."[5] That is right. The most exciting thing about the new birth is that our faith in Christ is His work and not our own, and therefore our salvation is securely established in Him.

John 3:16 shows that it is not enough to know what faith is; we must actually have it. There is a great divide in this world between those who perish and those who live forever. However, the line between those who are lost and those who are saved is not determined by who gives to charity, who observes certain religious rites, or even who is a little better than others in terms of moral conduct. The one thing that distinguishes those who perish forever and those who live forever is faith in Jesus. God gave Him to be our Savior, and salvation comes to all who believe—and only those who believe. There is one way of salvation—believing in Jesus Christ—and faith is therefore necessary for anyone to be saved.

Our Greatest Need: "Should Not Perish"

A number of years ago, Sproul wrote a book with a title that asked a vitally important question. It was *Saved from What?* He began by recounting a time almost forty years earlier when a stranger abruptly had stopped him and asked, "Are you saved?" Sproul was taken aback by the intrusion and responded with the first words that came into his mind: "Saved from what?" Here is a good question that every Christian witness should be able to answer. But the man who had stopped Sproul stammered and stuttered, unsure how to respond. As Sproul points out in his book, unless we know what we need to be saved *from*, we do not have an adequate understanding of the gospel and cannot truly share the Bible's message with others. He remembers: "Though this man had a zeal for salvation, he had little understanding of what salvation is. He was using Christian jargon. . . . But sadly, he had little understanding of what he was so zealously trying to communicate."[6]

The same cannot be said of the apostle John, who clearly presents the great peril from which we must be saved. God gave His Son, John says, so that "whoever believes in him should not perish."

According to John, our greatest need is to be saved from perishing. But what does *perish* mean? The best way to answer is to consider biblical statements that illuminate this teaching. For instance, there is Jesus' reference in this same chapter to the "serpent in the wilderness," which Moses lifted up (John 3:14). Jesus was referring to a deadly episode in Israel's history. During the exodus, the people had complained against God, so the Lord sent fiery serpents among them, and many people were bitten and died. This illustrates the warning in John 3:16 that without faith we will perish—that is, we will die.

Those snakes point back to the entry of sin into the world, when the Serpent tempted Adam and Eve to disobey God's command. God had warned them not to eat from the tree of the knowledge of good and evil, "for in the day that you eat of it you shall surely die" (Gen. 2:17b). When they disobeyed, however, they did not immediately die; instead, they were expelled from the garden and barred from the Tree of Life. In other words, they perished spiritually; physical death came later. Through their sin as our first parents, and through our own sins, the poison of death has entered our souls. Unless we are saved, we will experience everlasting death. To perish in this sense does not mean to cease to exist, but to be "tormented day and night forever" (Rev. 20:10b). Paul says that those who perish in their sins "will suffer the punishment of eternal destruction, away from the presence of the Lord and from the glory of his might" (2 Thess. 1:9).

This raises a question: How can a God who loves the world permit anyone to perish this way? Jesus answers, "Whoever believes in him is not condemned, but whoever does not believe is condemned already, because he has not believed in the name of the only Son of God" (John 3:18). The key word is *condemned*. The God who loves the world is also a perfectly holy judge. Abraham asked, "Shall not the Judge of all the earth do what is just?" (Gen. 18:25). The answer is yes! God's holy nature requires justice. This means that we must be judged for our sins unless they can be removed, the judgment being eternal death (see Rom. 6:23).

This is where God's love enters, because God showed His love for the world by sending His Son to die for our sins. God made a way for us to be forgiven and escape judgment, at infinite cost to Himself. This way requires that we receive God's Son in faith, so that our sins may be transferred to His account at the cross, where Jesus died as "the Lamb of God, who takes away the sin of the world" (John 1:29b). But if we spurn God's loving offer of salvation and refuse to believe on Jesus Christ, neither we nor God can avoid our condemnation. No unbeliever will suffer in hell because God lacked love, but "because he has not believed in the name of the only Son of God."

People resent the thought of God condemning anyone, especially them. But we have no cause to resent God. Jesus Himself revealed God's purpose in giving His Son to die for our sins: "For God did not send his Son into the world to condemn the world, but in order that the world might be saved through him" (John 3:17). God is never mean-spirited, even in His awful wrath. He has extended love to a world that is wicked, rebellious, and already condemned. God did not send Jesus to *cause* sinners to perish; sinners were going to perish without Jesus having to die. But God lovingly sent His Son to pay with His own blood the sin-debt for all who believe. God is like a doctor who prescribes the healing medicine. But if we refuse to admit our sickness and refuse to take the pills, we condemn ourselves to death. So it is with all who refuse to receive Jesus as Savior and Lord.

John's Gospel describes Jesus as a light shining in the world—and that shining has inescapable consequences. Morris reminds us:

> It is not the purpose of the shining of the sun to cast shadows. But . . . shadows are inevitable. The shadows are, so to speak, the other side of the sunshine. So it is with condemnation and the coming of the Son of God. He did not come in order that people be condemned. But there are great moral issues involved,

and those who refuse salvation thus condemn themselves. The condemnation is as real as the salvation.[7]

"Saved from what?" The Bible assures us that our greatest need is to be saved from the wrath of God, saved from the just condemnation our sins deserve, and saved from perishing in everlasting death. One of the tragedies of the Titanic, the great ocean liner that sank with the loss of so many lives, was the number of empty seats on the lifeboats taking people to safety. A greater tragedy is the unclaimed offer of God to save us from eternal death through faith in His only Son.

Our Greatest Blessing: "But Have Eternal Life"

In His love for the world, God gave His Son not only to meet our greatest need, but to offer us the greatest possible blessing. Jesus completed His gospel summary with these words: "For God so loved the world, that he gave his only Son, that whoever believes in him should not perish *but have eternal life*" (John 3:16, emphasis added). God saves us *from* perishing in our sins and *to* eternal life in His glory.

As with *perish*, we should define *eternal life* in keeping with the teaching of Jesus in this chapter and in John's Gospel generally. *Eternal life* obviously speaks of a quantity of life—believers in Jesus will live everlastingly into the future. Jesus said: "I am the resurrection and the life. Whoever believes in me, though he die, yet shall he live, and everyone who lives and believes in me shall never die" (John 11:25–26). Those who believe in Jesus will participate in His resurrection life. They may die as a result of accidents, sickness, or old age. But Jesus has removed the sting of death from believers—He has taken away its condemnation and has overcome its effects—just as the poison of the snakebites was removed from those Israelites who looked to the serpent Moses lifted up (John 3:14). For one who believes in Christ, death is a gateway into a new life that will never end.

But *eternal life* is not only about the quantity of life believers enjoy. It also speaks to the quality of life that begins as soon as we believe. John writes, "Whoever believes in the Son has eternal life" (John 3:36a). Notice the present tense of that statement. Believers possess eternal life as soon as and because we believe in Jesus. This truth connects with Jesus' earlier teaching, when He spoke of us being "born again" and "seeing" the kingdom of God (John 3:3). He also said we can be "born of the Spirit" (John 3:8). These sayings describe eternal life. One of the most famous Puritan books was titled *The Life of God in the Soul of Man,* and that is an excellent description for eternal life.[8] A poet said of another Puritan, Richard Sibbes, "Of this blest man, let this just praise be given, Heaven was in him, before he was in heaven."[9] Eternal life is a life of spiritual understanding and vitality, a life in which God's own Spirit moves within us, and a life of seeing and even entering God's kingdom of grace and light. Paul said that the kingdom of God consists in "righteousness and peace and joy in the Holy Spirit" (Rom. 14:17b). Those are qualities of eternal life.

Does this truth not highlight the preciousness, the necessity, and the urgency of faith in Christ? In His great love, God saves us *from* perishing, *to* eternal life, *through* faith in His only Son. What money can never buy, what works can never earn, what tears can never inspire, God gives to those who believe in His Son. This being true, we ought to repent of any unbelief and turn to Christ in faith. We should guard and nurture our faith through God's Word and prayer. If we struggle to believe, we should come to God humbly, as Jesus' disciples did, asking, "Increase our faith!" (Luke 17:5). The God who loved us enough to send His only Son will not fail to send the Holy Spirit to strengthen the faith by which alone we can be saved.

"Life! Life! Eternal Life!"

John Bunyan brilliantly depicted salvation through faith in Christ in his great book *The Pilgrim's Progress.* His hero, Christian, discovered that his great need was to avoid perishing in his sins. A man advised him to "Fly from the wrath to come." So Christian began running, crying out, "Life! Life! Eternal life!" People thought he was a lunatic, just as they think of Christians today. Some friends tried to stop him. Running after him, they reminded him of all that he was forsaking. But Christian invited them to join him, explaining: "All which you shall forsake is not worthy to be compared with a little of that that I am seeking to enjoy. . . . I seek an inheritance incorruptible, undefiled, and that fadeth not away; and it is laid up in heaven, and safe there, to be bestowed . . . on them that diligently seek it." Though they refused and went back, Christian pressed on in faith.[10]

Bunyan's tale is so valuable because he understood the message of John 3:16 so well. Christian fled from destruction toward eternal life. And he ran not just anywhere, but to a narrow gate beyond which a light was shining. Beyond the gate, Christian came to a cross. As he looked at that cross—like Israel gazing to Moses' serpent lifted up—the burden on his back (the weight of his many sins) came sliding off and fell away forever. There he gained the right to enter the Celestial City. At the end of his journey, as Christian drew near to that city, the angels came and told him: "You are going now to the paradise of God, wherein you shall see the tree of life, and eat of the never-fading fruits thereof. . . . You shall have white robes given you, and your walk and talk shall be every day with the King, even all the days of eternity."[11] Bunyan describes Christian and his companion, Hopeful, going into the heavenly city through the gates: "And lo, as they entered, they were transfigured, and they had raiment put on that shone like gold. . . . All the bells in the city rang again for joy, and it was said unto them, 'Enter ye into the joy of your Lord.'"[12]

The Pilgrim's Progress tells a story that is thrilling to Christians because it depicts what is true for us. One crucial part of the truth of the story is that Bunyan's Christian journeyed to the cross and from there to the Celestial City because someone told him where to go. The man's name, predictably, was Evangelist. Early in the book, this man found Christian standing still with tears in his eyes. Evangelist inquired about him and found that the poor man had realized his need for salvation and was weeping over the certain judgment of his soul. "If this is your condition," Evangelist asked him, "why are you standing still?" Christian replied, "Because I do not know where to go."[13]

Thankfully for Bunyan's Christian, Evangelist knew what to tell him. Do you know? If our witness is to lead others to eternal life, we must be able to direct them to Jesus Christ and His cross through a true and saving faith. And if we do, those who believe will not perish but will have eternal life.

NOTES

[1] R. C. Sproul, *Faith Alone: The Evangelical Doctrine of Justification* (Grand Rapids, Mich.: Baker Books, 1995), 78.

[2] Leon Morris, *Expository Reflections on the Letter to the Ephesians* (Grand Rapids, Mich.: Baker Books, 1994), 97.

[3] James Montgomery Boice, *Foundations of the Christian Faith* (Downers Grove, Ill.: InterVarsity Press, 1986), 414.

[4] C. H. Dodd, *The Interpretation of the Fourth Gospel* (Cambridge, England: Cambridge University Press, 1968), 179–186.

[5] Joseph "Skip" Ryan, *That You May Believe* (Wheaton, Ill.: Crossway Books, 2003), 103.

[6] R. C. Sproul, *Saved from What?* (Wheaton, Ill.: Crossway Books, 2002), 13–14.

[7] Leon Morris, *Reflections on the Gospel of John* (Peabody, Mass.: Hendrickson Publishers, 1986), 102.

[8] Henry Scougal, *The Life of God in the Soul of Man* (Harrisonburg, Va.: Sprinkle Publications, 1986).

[9] Izaak Walton, cited in *Works of Richard Sibbes*, 7 vols. (Edinburgh, Scotland, and Carlisle, Pa.: Banner of Truth Trust, 1973), 1:xx.

[10] John Bunyan, *The Pilgrim's Progress* (Grand Rapids, Mich.: Baker Books, 1984), 11–13.

[11] Ibid., 197.

[12] Ibid., 200–201.

[13] Ibid., 12.

Questions for discussion and reflection:

1. What are the three elements of saving faith? Why is each of them essential for salvation?

2. How would you explain to another person why faith in Jesus is the greatest possession anyone could have? Are there any Bible passages you love that help make the point?

3. How does the word *amen* summarize saving faith? How does the idea of marriage help to explain the meaning of faith?

4. Some Christians say that we should "forget theology" and just "get people saved." Why is this idea dangerous? What are we saved *from*? Why must our gospel witness make this clear?

5. Should the topic of hell come up in our witness? If a friend were to ask you, "How could a loving God send people to hell?" how would you respond? What really condemns a person to hell?

6. How would you explain the meaning of "eternal life"? How is this teaching related to the doctrine of Christ's resurrection?

PART THREE

Jesus' Witness to
the Samaritan Woman:

Jesus' Practice of Evangelism

Chapter 9

JESUS THE EVANGELIST

John 4:1–10

Jesus answered her, "If you knew the gift of God, and who it is that is saying to you, 'Give me a drink,' you would have asked him, and he would have given you living water."

—*John 4:10*

It would be hard to find a more interesting array of individuals than that which is presented in the Gospel of John. We have most of the famous figures from the Gospels: Jesus, the twelve disciples, Mary, and John the Baptist. But ordinary people also stroll through John, and in them we see many fascinating details of human life. They are all different, but also much the same. Through them, John proves to us that the gospel is for everyone. Jesus came to save not a certain class or type of person, but all kinds of people, each of whom must receive Him only in faith.

It is particularly interesting to contrast and compare Nicodemus, featured in John 3, with the woman at the well in John 4. Nicodemus was a man at the top of life, one admired by almost everyone, but one who needed to be born again. But lest we should think that only the proud need salvation, we are next introduced to someone at the other end of life. Here was an immoral woman who, because of her bad reputation, had to fetch water from the well in the heat of the day, when the other women were gone. James Montgomery Boice comments:

> It is difficult to imagine a greater contrast between two persons than the contrast between the important and sophisticated Nicodemus, this ruler of the Jews, and the simple Samaritan woman. He was a Jew; she a Samaritan. He was a Pharisee; she belonged to no religious party. He was a politician; she had no status whatever. He was a scholar; she was uneducated. He was highly moral; she was immoral. He had a name; she is nameless. He was a man; she was a woman. He came at night, to protect his reputation; she, who had no reputation, came at noon. Nicodemus came seeking; the woman was sought by Jesus.
>
> A great contrast. Yet the point of the stories is that both the man and the woman needed the gospel and were welcome to it. If Nicodemus is an example of the truth that no one can rise so high as to be above salvation, the woman is an example of the truth that none can sink too low.[1]

There can be little doubt that John placed these two figures side by side to show that the gospel is for everyone. Because of unbelief, not everyone in the world *is* saved. But the glory of the gospel is that anyone—regardless of gender, race, education, wealth, or social position—*may* be saved through faith in Jesus Christ.

As we begin to study John 4, we approach a complete understanding of John's portrayal of Jesus the Evangelist. Chapter 1 provided us with rich general principles for witnessing the gospel. Jesus' encounter with Nicodemus in Chapter 3 laid out the theological message of the gospel. Now, as Jesus sits beside the Samaritan woman at the well, we observe His practice of evangelism. What approach characterized Jesus' witness to ordinary people? What was His attitude to sinful people in need of the gospel? What logic did Jesus employ in seeking a hearing for His message of God's grace? Jesus' witness to the Samaritan woman is a gold mine in our search for an evangelistic method, for here our Lord Himself sets us an example of speaking the truth in love.

Caring for the Lost

If it glorifies Jesus that He makes salvation possible for everyone, it glorifies Him even more that He actually saves particular individuals. Christian salvation is universal in its offer but particular in its application. A great example of this comes in the account of how Jesus went out of His way to bring His gospel to the woman at the well and, through her, to an entire village. Here we see Jesus the Evangelist bringing the gospel to those whom He would save.

John 4 contains a number of famous statements, but the most glorious may be the one in verse 4. John begins this chapter by telling us that Jesus started gathering followers, who were baptized by the twelve disciples, and then He "left Judea and departed again for Galilee" (John 4:3). John then says: "And he had to pass through Samaria" (John 4:4). What makes this statement so wonderful is the way in which it was *not* true. Geographically, Jesus did not have to pass through Samaria, and for many reasons it was inconvenient for Him to do so. But John informs us that Jesus *had* to go this way; it was necessary for Him. The reason was Jesus' determination to save His own, among whom was this woman by the well.

Donald Grey Barnhouse once compared this detour by Jesus to a soldier who returns from overseas and travels from San Francisco to his home in Philadelphia. Along the way, he *has* to stop in Miami. Why is such a detour needed? He answers, "Because my fiancée lives there!" Likewise, Jesus was compelled to go through Samaria because of love.

In this chapter, we will examine the features of Jesus' evangelistic approach. The first of these is *caring for the lost*.

Serving the gospel is always hard work, and so it was for Jesus. Such was His care for others that He wearied Himself bringing the gospel to them. He traveled a long road through Samaria. When He arrived at the town of Sychar, John tells us, "Jacob's well was there; so Jesus, wearied as He was from His journey, was sitting beside the well" (John 4:6). Likewise, if we care for others' salvation, we will expend ourselves in ministry to them—in prayer, in service, and in witness. If we are not willing to be wearied—if we do not find ourselves sometimes needing a rest from our labors—then we are not likely to accomplish much in Christian ministry.

The apostle John wrote this Gospel in part to persuade us of Jesus' deity. But scenes like this display Jesus' full humanity. As the Son of God, He was completely self-sufficient. But as a man, Jesus grew tired and thirsty. He needed rest and something to drink. When you pray about the weariness of life and the hardships you endure, Jesus knows what you mean, because He has been weary, too.

Many of us are ineffective evangelists simply because we are too lazy and self-centered. We are not willing to cross the street to meet people. We do not care enough for the eternal destiny of friends, family members, and co-workers to risk the social hazard of talking about the Lord. Our lives are focused on our own needs and those of our children, so we have no time to participate in outreach ministries. For many of us, the first step in doing evangelism is simply to care enough for the lost to become weary in the gospel. Those who do tire themselves in gospel outreach have sweet fellowship with the Savior who rested at the well.

One way to motivate yourself to care for others is to realize how much Jesus sacrificed to care for your own soul. We see His particular concern for individuals in His journey through Samaria. Had Jesus merely wanted to open a way for salvation for whoever would come, He need never have gone to Samaria. What He soon was to do in Jerusalem—namely, His death on the cross for our sins—was sufficient to make a way to God. Jesus did not have to go to Samaria for this. But Jesus died not only generally for all who would come, but actually to save particular people known to Him, including the woman He knew was coming to draw water from this well.

If you are a believer, the same is true of you. Just as Jesus personally brought the gospel to the Samaritan woman, so He personally sought you for salvation. If you have heard the gospel and believed, it was not by chance! Jesus cared for *your* soul, so He died on the cross for *your* sins, He sent His witnesses to *you*, and He commissioned the Holy Spirit to open *your* heart to believe. "You did not choose me, but I chose you," He said (John 15:16). Realizing His sacrificial care for your soul ought to inspire you to care for the salvation of people you know and love, that He might send you as His witness to them.

Crossing the Boundaries

Evangelism requires a caring motivation. But as Jesus' example shows, the next step in sharing the gospel is *crossing the boundaries* that separate people from God. This Samaritan woman never would have come to Jerusalem, where Jesus had been preaching and working miracles; she knew she would not fit in among the Jews. So Jesus crossed the boundaries and went to her. John tells us:

> There came a woman of Samaria to draw water. Jesus said to her, "Give me a drink." (For his disciples had gone away into the city to buy food.) The Samaritan woman said to him, "How is it that you, a Jew, ask for a drink from me, a woman of Samaria?" (For Jews have no dealings with Samaritans.) (John 4:7–9)

In this brief exchange, Jesus crossed three barriers. The first was that which separated Samaritans from Jews. In the eighth century BC, the Assyrian Empire conquered the northern kingdom of Israel and deported the Israelites who lived there. In their place, the Assyrians brought other peoples to populate the land (see 2 Kings 17:24). These Gentiles sought to worship both the gods of their homelands and the local deity, the God of the Israelites, so they mixed the religions. This was a grave offense to the Jews, and over the centuries their hatred only grew as the Samaritans developed their own brand of Judaism. Because of this resentment, most Jews traveling between Jerusalem and

Galilee went the long way around Samaria and carefully avoided personal contact with Samaritan people. Rabbi Eliezer taught, "He that eats the bread of the Samaritans is like to one that eats the flesh of swine."[2] So the first barrier Jesus crossed was a barrier of ethnic and cultural hatred.

This Samaritan was also a woman. It may not seem scandalous to us for a man to sit at a well with a woman, but it certainly was in Jesus' day. Religious Jewish men used to thank God daily that they had not been born Samaritans, but they also prayed, "Blessed art thou, O Lord ... who hast not made me a woman." A rabbi would lose his reputation if he spoke publicly to any woman, even his own wife or daughter. Yet Jesus unashamedly crossed that gender barrier.

Third, Jesus overcame a social and religious taboo by asking for a drink. Jews did not share utensils with Samaritans; doing so risked separation from the fellowship and worship of God's people under the temple rules. But Jesus deliberately crossed that line, too. Even the woman was astonished by this, asking, "How is it that you, a Jew, ask for a drink from me, a woman of Samaria?" (v. 9).

Why did Jesus cross these barriers? Because He cared for the woman's soul. We, too, have to cross barriers to reach people for Christ. This does not mean that we should participate in sin—Jesus never did that. But it does mean that we have to reach out to people who will never come to church or read the Bible. This woman did not belong in the religious world that produced Jesus. So He came into her world with the gospel. He crossed ethnic, gender, and religious lines to seek her out. William Barclay exclaims, "Here is God so loving the world, not in theory, but in action."[3] We must do the same on His behalf.

In His exchange with Nicodemus, Jesus gave us a very negative explanation for unbelief: He said that people love darkness and hate light (John 3:19), so they have no interest in Christ. But more of the story is shown in John 4. Many people are kept from God simply because they think they don't belong at church. They assume that believers will look down on them. Moreover, they feel uncomfortable in religious surroundings, the way a Samaritan would have felt in Jerusalem. For all these reasons, they are not likely to come to us, so we have to take the gospel to them.

When I think back to the circumstances under which I came to Christ, I realize how unlikely it was, humanly speaking. Though I was raised in a moral and religious home, I did not have biblical beliefs. I was really a secular humanist. The truths taught by the Bible were contemptible to me. The lives led by Christians held little appeal to my heart. I would not, on my own, have crossed the threshold of a church to meet with Jesus Christ. So Jesus crossed the threshold to me and sat down by the well of my heart. He created a thirst for truth and meaning. He sent witnesses to cross my path. When I first responded to the gospel, He sent authentic Christians to befriend and encourage me. Jesus crossed the boundaries I never would have crossed; I would not have come into His world, so He came into my world and drew me to Himself. Likewise, Jesus often sits at the well waiting for people we know and desiring for them to hear the gospel through our lips.

Connecting with People

Even crossing multiple barriers merely brought Jesus into contact with this woman. His next step involved *connecting* with her on a personal level.

We find out in this chapter that the Samaritan woman was a sinful person who held all kinds of false beliefs, just as many people do today. However, Jesus did not treat her as a pariah, but as a person. He started with a simple request —"Give me a drink"—that sparked a connection. We might think that He should have opened the encounter with a display of miraculous power to awe her—perhaps making the water flow up the well to fill His cup. Or perhaps He should have rebuked her for the mess that her life undoubtedly was. But Jesus thought it wiser to humble Himself in His true humanity and give her an opportunity to minister to His need.

Many Christians today wall themselves off from the world the way the Jews of Jesus' time did. Just as the Jews chose to bypass Samaria to avoid defilement, we tend to travel only within our own subculture. If we interact with worldly people, we certainly don't think they have anything to offer us. Small wonder, then, that they are not open to what we have to offer them. Jesus was not like that: He walked through the world and treated even a scandalous Samaritan woman as a person of worth, capable of giving Him something of value. As Frederick Godet wisely notes, "He is not unaware that the way to gain a soul is often to ask a service of it."[4]

Vastly superior as Jesus was to this woman, He placed Himself in her care. By exposing her to His need, He opened the door to a relationship in which meaningful content could be exchanged. Christians today need to see this, for we hinder our witness if we cultivate a façade that masks our weaknesses, struggles, and needs. There are skills we lack that our neighbors can offer and matters on which we can turn to them for advice. We should not hide our anxiety, fear, and grief from non-Christians. Being Christian makes us not less human but more human, and we can connect with people by living authentically in all our weakness, displaying Christ's power through our faith. Our example is the Lord Almighty, who did not hide His weariness from the Samaritan woman; He who offered living water was not ashamed to say, "Give me a drink." J. C. Ryle comments: "Simple as this request may seem, it opened a door to spiritual conversation. It threw a bridge across the gulf which lay between her and Him. It led to the conversion of her soul."[5]

It is my opinion that Jesus came to this well knowing this woman would be there. Given His divine omniscience, He must have known; therefore, He came specifically for her. He even seems to have waited in thirst until she should come along and give Him the pail. This reminds us that the doctrine of election is no deterrent to evangelism but a motivation—we know God has people around us to be saved, so we witness with confidence. And, like Jesus, we should have specific people on our hearts for whom we are praying and with whom we are seeking to share the gospel. Yet God in His sovereignty can send anyone to us at any time to hear about Jesus and be saved. Knowing this, we should look upon every encounter as a divine appointment and seek to make a connection through which we may talk about Jesus and the gospel.

The woman at the well was so astonished by Jesus' approach to her that she gave Him an immediate opportunity to share the gospel: "The Samaritan woman said to him, 'How is it that you, a Jew, ask for a drink from me, a woman of Samaria?'" (John 4:9a). Likewise, unbelieving people who live next door to Christians, who work alongside Christians, or whose family members are converted to Christian faith ought to be compelled to ask us what makes us different. They ought to observe a sincere godliness in our conduct, a graciousness in our speech, and a compassion and concern in our hearts—all of which are in decreasing supply today—so that they ask us to tell them what Christ has done in our lives.

Communicating Good News

Relating to and connecting with people have been called "pre-evangelism" because, as important as these activities are, we have not actually evangelized until we tell people about the salvation God offers. Jesus followed up His opportunity by clearly and directly *communicating good news* to the Samaritan woman: "Jesus answered her, 'If you knew the gift of God, and who it is that is saying to you, "Give me a drink," you would have asked him, and he would have given you living water'" (John 4:10).

We will study Jesus' description of salvation more carefully in the next chapter, but we should first make some observations about the way Jesus presented the gospel. First, He used the situation He was in to point to spiritual realities. After feeding the five thousand with a few loaves, Jesus spoke of Himself as the bread of life (John 6:35). After the light festival in Jerusalem, He called out, "I am the light of the world" (John 8:12). Here by the well, He made the analogy between the thirst of the body and the thirst of the soul, so as to offer the living waters of eternal life.

Second, Jesus pointedly spoke of the gift God offers. He began, "If you knew the gift of God. . . ." The point of evangelism is that people do not know the gospel. People have no idea that God has something to give them. They little imagine—though their hearts yearn for it—that there is more to life than this work-a-day world and its unsatisfying recreations. It never occurs to them that God looks on them with care and grace to save if only they will ask. Most people look on God with the vague resentment this woman first cast toward Jesus; in her eyes, He was an authority to be resisted and a judge to be avoided. They do not know the gift of God; we have the privilege of telling them.

The heart of our gospel is good news about God's free gift. Jesus communicates this same good news to you today through the Gospel of John. Jesus cares for your soul, so He came from heaven to earth to sit down at the well by your heart and meet personally with you. He came to offer you the greatest gift imaginable. God offers Christ's blood to wash away your sins so that you may stand righteous in His sight. He offers His Holy Spirit to take up residence in your heart, light casting out darkness, truth evicting error, holiness subduing the cravings of sin. He offers you life beyond the grave, the resurrection body that Paul describes as imperishable, glorious, and heavenly (1 Cor. 15:42–49). But towering above all these inestimable gifts, God offers you Himself. "I will be your God, and you shall be my people," He says (Jer. 7:23). How terrible it would be for us to spurn God's gift. In Jeremiah's day, God lamented the folly of those who rejected Him for the unfulfilling drink of worldliness and sin: "They have forsaken me, the fountain of living waters, and hewed out cisterns for themselves, broken cisterns that can hold no water" (Jer. 2:13). But the psalmist speaks for those who have known God's gift through Jesus Christ: "In your presence there is fullness of joy; at your right hand are pleasures forevermore" (Ps. 16:11).

God created us with a thirst that only He can quench by the living waters Jesus offers through faith. Jesus said, "I came that they may have life and have it abundantly" (John 10:10). And by inspiring us to care for the salvation of others, cross the boundaries, and connect with people around us, God wants to communicate this same good news to all kinds of people in this world—people like Nicodemus, the Samaritan woman, and every other kind of person. Jesus said, "As the Father has sent me, even so I am sending you" (John 20:21).

NOTES

1 James Montgomery Boice, *The Gospel of John*, 5 vols. (Grand Rapids, Mich.: Baker Books, 1999), 1:272.

2 Cited from Leon Morris, *Reflections on the Gospel of John* (Peabody, Mass.: Hendrickson Publishers, 1986), 126.

3 William Barclay, *The Gospel of John*, 2 vols. (Philadelphia, Pa.: Westminster, 1975), 1:151.

4 Frederick Louis Godet, *Commentary on the Gospel of John* (Grand Rapids, Mich.: Zondervan, 1893), 1:422.

5 J. C. Ryle, *Expository Thoughts on the Gospels: John*, 3 vols. (Edinburgh, Scotland, and Carlisle, Pa.: Banner of Truth Trust, 1999), 1:203.

Questions for discussion and reflection:

1. What two types of people are represented by Nicodemus and the Samaritan woman? In what ways are they different? How are they similar? How does Jesus touch each of them personally with the gospel?

2. In what ways was the Samaritan woman an outcast in her day? How does her life depict the effects of sin?

3. What are the four points of Jesus' evangelistic example? How might these shape your approach to sharing the gospel?

4. What barriers did Jesus cross in order to reach the Samaritan woman? What barriers do you face in your own witness? What are some wrong ways in which Christians sometimes try to cross barriers? Does barrier-crossing require us to change the message of the gospel?

5. Jesus was deliberate in connecting with the woman by the well on a personal level. What opportunities do you have to connect with non-Christians? How can you be more deliberate in establishing a personal relationship that might lead to someone's salvation?

6. What two things did Jesus focus on in communicating the good news? Are they both essential? If so, why? How does it encourage our witness to see how boldly Jesus offered salvation as a free gift?

7. Use Jesus' approach to the Samaritan woman as a guide to prayer. Ask God to give you a caring heart for the lost. Ask Him to make you wise and bold in crossing boundaries, and loving in making a personal connection. Then ask God to use your offer of the salvation gift to lead someone else to eternal life.

Chapter 10

LIVING WATER

John 4:10–15

"Everyone who drinks of this water will be thirsty again, but whoever drinks of the water that I will give him will never be thirsty forever. The water that I will give him will become in him a spring of water welling up to eternal life."

—*John 4:13–14*

In 1509, Don Diego Columbus arrived on the island of Hispaniola to rule as the Spanish governor in the West Indies. Don Diego, son of the great explorer Christopher Columbus, arrived with several relatives, a large retinue of cavaliers, and a troop of well-bred ladies sent to marry and civilize the leading colonists of New Spain. Among those colonists was Juan Ponce de Leon, governor of Puerto Rico. Ponce had distinguished himself in battle and was revered as a personal companion of Christopher Columbus. Though an old man, he was still motivated by the ambitions of youth. Thus, he watched in frustration as the younger courtiers took their young wives and set off for wealth and renown. One biographer says, "The enjoyment of life had ever been an exquisite pleasure to him, and his desire to prolong his earthly existence in vigor was intense."[1]

Because of this desire, Ponce was inspired by legends of "crystal waters flowing from living springs . . . in which he who bathed would be instantly endowed with immortal youth and great beauty."[2] Outfitting a small fleet, he began searching for this "Fountain of Youth." Being first directed to the Bahama Islands, he bathed in every stream and lake there. Disappointed, he extended his search to the northwest. On Easter Sunday, 1513, he landed at what is now the city of St. Augustine, having been drawn there by the perfume of flowers wafting over the ocean. Believing himself to have discovered paradise, he claimed the land for Spain and named it *Florida* in honor of the flowers. Certain that the Fountain of Youth must be among the magnolia-lined streams nearby, and anxious to taste the promised golden fruit proffered by the hands of lovely maidens, Ponce searched in earnest but also in vain. Finally, frustrated at his failure to find the fountain, he returned to Puerto Rico having gained not immortal youth but immortal fame for discovering Florida and for seeking eternal life.[3]

Jesus' Offer of Living Water

If Ponce de Leon had read his Bible instead of listening to native legends, he would have known that the fountain of eternal life was not to be found in the Bahamas or in Florida. In fact, it had been revealed centuries earlier at an ancient well outside the town of Sychar in Samaria. But according to Jesus, Jacob's well, beside which He sat with the Samaritan woman, was not the source of living water. Rather, Jesus Himself was and is the fountain of eternal life. "If you knew the gift of God," He said, "and who it is that is saying to you, 'Give me a drink,' you would have asked him, and he would have given you living water" (John 4:10). Then, pointing to the well, He added, "Everyone who drinks of this water will be thirsty again, but whoever drinks of the water that I will give him will never be thirsty forever" (John 4:13–14a). Though lacking the scented flowers, the golden apples, and the lovely maidens of the legend, here was a fountain of youth and vigor from which Ponce de Leon might have drunk without sailing about in ships, and from which any one of us may benefit simply by believing in Jesus Christ.

In His conversation with the woman at the well, Jesus made use of the link between water and life. Water is absolutely necessary for life in this world. If you fly over the Great Plains in the central United States, you look down on a brown landscape slashed with green lines and dotted with green squares and circles. The lines are rivers, where water flows; the squares and circles are farmlands watered by irrigation systems. Where there is water, there is life. Along these lines, Jesus was using His earthly situation, sitting by a well, to make a point about spiritual life. As a well gives water for our bodies, so God gives life to our souls.

In Jesus' day, the expression *living water* referred to fresh, running water, in contrast to the stagnant water found in wells. But those who are familiar with the Bible also see this as a reference to the gift of abundant life through the Holy Spirit that God promised through the Messiah. In Jeremiah 2:13, God described Himself as "the fountain of living waters." Psalm 36:9a says, "For with you is the fountain of life." Isaiah 44:3 tells of the coming day of salvation: "For I will pour water on the thirsty land, and streams on the dry ground; I will pour out my Spirit on your offspring." The last book of the Bible, Revelation, depicts "the river of the water of life" flowing from the throne of God and of His Son, the Savior-Lamb (Rev. 22:1). One writer therefore describes living water as "the soul-satisfying grace of God, or that which only God can give to satisfy a soul. It is . . . the transforming life and power that God alone gives in and through the gospel of His Son, that leads to eternal life, and that satisfies as nothing else can."[4]

In making His offer of salvation to the Samaritan woman, Jesus summarized His entire gospel in terms of two things the world needs to know. First, He said, "If you knew the gift of God . . ." (John 4:10a). This is what we need to know: God has life as a gift for those who will receive it. God says, "Come, everyone who thirsts, come to the waters" (Isa. 55:1a), and we may bring the parched soil of our hearts to Him that He might water it. Second, Jesus said, "If you knew . . . who it is that is saying to you, 'Give me a drink' . . ." (John 4:10a). We need to know who Jesus is—the Savior sent by God to bring eternal life to a dying world. In these two statements is our whole gospel; in order to be saved, we and others need to know what the gift of God is and who Jesus is as the One who brings it. We must ask of Him, and He will bring eternal life as living water for our souls. We need *it*—God's gift of eternal life—from *Him*—the Savior, Jesus Christ. Jesus promised: "If you knew the gift of God, and who it is that is saying to you, 'Give me a drink,' you would have asked him, and he would have given you living water" (John 4:10).

Unquenched Thirst

Jesus' offer produced a revealing response from the woman: "The woman said to him, 'Sir, you have nothing to draw water with, and the well is deep. Where do you get that living water?'" (John 4:11). Here we have another depiction of unbelief. We saw in John 3:19 that unbelief is caused by a moral commitment to sin: Jesus said, "Light has come into the world, and people loved the darkness rather than the light because their deeds were evil." We also observed that there are barriers that keep many people from believing in God—cultural, ethnic, and religious barriers—all of which Jesus crossed in speaking to this Samaritan woman. Now, in her response, we see yet another reason for unbelief: spiritual inability. The woman simply was not able to grasp what Jesus meant in His offer of salvation. She was an earthly, worldly person, unable to think in spiritual terms.

The Bible teaches that fallen mankind is dead to spiritual things (see Eph. 2:1–3). Paul says, "The natural person does not accept the things of the Spirit of God, for they are folly to him, and he is *not able* to understand them because they are spiritually discerned" (1 Cor. 2:14, emphasis added). This woman was a perfect example of this teaching, for she could think only in terms of physical water and literal wells. Nicodemus was similarly unable to understand Jesus in John 3. Jesus said to him, "Unless one is born again he *cannot* see the kingdom of

God" (John 3:3, emphasis added), to which Nicodemus responded with a question about reentering the womb, revealing his lack of understanding.

The woman's reply to Jesus was almost as comical as Nicodemus's. She did not see how He could offer what she understood only as running water. First, Jesus had no pail: "Sir, you have nothing to draw water with, and the well is deep. Where do you get that living water?" (John 4:11). Second, she could not see how Jesus could do better than so great a man as the patriarch Jacob: "Are you greater than our father Jacob? He gave us the well and drank from it himself, as did his sons and his livestock" (John 4:12). Jacob's well remains in Samaria today; it is over one hundred feet deep and was likely deeper then. Some scholars believe Jacob's well may have been the deepest in all of Palestine.[5] How could this stranger—a man with no apparent distinction or station—hope to do better than Jacob and his well?

People think the same way today. Jesus is not someone they take seriously because He does not head a powerful organization or command worldly resources. The people who matter, they think, are those who allocate riches and promotions, or who provide valued goods and services. Despite His unparalleled religious status, Jesus is thought to be of little earthly good—and most people think only of earthly things, as did this Samaritan woman. Jesus did not bring any advanced technology, so He simply could not compare with people who really mattered—like Jacob, who at least was the forefather of a great nation. She was interested in plumbing, not salvation; she wanted an easier way to get better water from the well. Likewise, people today want advice on relationships, work, and play, not theological "jargon" about Jesus.

The problem with such thinking goes back to Jesus' offer: "If you knew the gift of God, and who it is that is speaking to you . . ." (John 4:10). The truth is that the spiritual realm is superior to the material realm; God's gift of spiritual life is more valuable than earthly riches. Moreover, though Jesus Christ seems so easy to dismiss, in fact God has "seated him at his right hand in the heavenly places, far above all rule and authority and power and dominion, and above every name that is named, not only in this age but also in the one to come. And he put all things under his feet" (Eph. 1:20b–22a). Even in earthly matters—such as our jobs, families, and health—where human powers can affect us, Jesus has ultimate authority. But, more important, Jesus has authority over our eternal souls. Unless we come to Him in faith, we are condemned already for not believing in the name of God's only Son, as Jesus Himself makes clear (John 3:18).

Does this truth not inspire us to tell people what they do not know? This woman of Samaria had many problems. She needed help with her relationships, with the stress of being rejected by other women, and with the simple task of getting water from this well, along with many other difficulties. But her greatest need was to be reconciled to God through Jesus Christ. This is why we must preach the gospel. We are not called to give lifestyle tips or the self-help plumbing that today's worldly men and women crave. The Bible says the gospel "is the power of God for salvation to everyone who believes" (Rom. 1:16b), so we must proclaim it.

With this in mind, Jesus replied to the woman, "Everyone who drinks of this water will be thirsty again" (John 4:13). Every earthly source of life and fulfillment will fail to satisfy our souls. Even if the woman had gotten beautiful pipes that could bring the well water all the way to her house, she still would have thirsted again. However, she had a deeper, more profound thirst that she didn't even recognize. The souls of men and women are thirsty for God, whether they know it or not. Nothing except God can satisfy the soul made by God for Himself. St. Augustine wrote at the beginning of his *Confessions*: "You have made us for yourself, and our heart is restless until it rests in you."[6] Psalm 42:1 speaks for us all: "As a deer pants for flowing streams, so pants my soul for you, O God."

This was true for the Samaritan woman and it is true for you. You may have all this world can offer—riches, rank, place, and power—yet be utterly unfulfilled. Isn't this the story of our time? Amidst gaudy affluence and ever-ready entertainment, with unparalleled leisure and earthly excitements, ours is a generation aching with thirst. Arthur W. Pink summarizes the human condition:

> Whether he articulates it or not the natural man, the world over, is crying "I thirst." Why this consuming desire to acquire wealth? Why this craving for the honors and plaudits of the world? Why this mad rush after pleasure, the turning from one form of it to another with persistent and unwearied diligence? Why this eager search for wisdom—this scientific inquiry, this pursuit of philosophy, this ransacking of the writings of the ancients, and this ceaseless experimentation by the moderns? Why the insane craze for that which is novel? Why? Because there is an aching void in the soul. Because there is something remaining in every natural man that is *unsatisfied*. This is true of the millionaire equally as much as the pauper: the riches of the former bring no real contentment. It is as true of the globe-trotter equally as much as of the country rustic who has never been outside the bounds of his native country: traveling from one end of the earth to the other and back again fails to discover the secret of peace. Over all the cisterns of this world's providing is written in letters of ineffaceable truth, "Whosoever drinks of this water *shall thirst again*."[7]

Remember Ponce de Leon? The tragedy of his life was not that he never found the Fountain of Youth. The tragedy was that even if he had found it, its unending earthly pleasures would not have satisfied him.

So what are you seeking? Riches? Pleasure? Fame? People today seek these things diligently, but find no satisfaction when they gain them. Jesus says that whatever earthly fulfillment you may find, you will only thirst again. Especially when our seeking leads us into sin, we end up like broken cisterns—not even capable of being satisfied, no longer even able to hold water, unless Christ should come and heal our souls.

Malcolm Muggeridge was one of the leading journalists and writers of his generation. Through the thirst of his soul, he learned what Jesus sought to communicate to this Samaritan woman. He reflected:

> I may . . . pass for being a relatively successful man. People occasionally stare at me in the streets—that's fame. I can fairly easily earn enough to qualify for admission to the higher slopes of the Inland Revenue—that's success. Furnished with money and a little fame . . . [I] may partake of trendy diversions—that's pleasure. It might happen once in a while that something I said or wrote . . . represented a serious impact on our time—that's fulfillment. Yet I say to you, and I beg you to believe me, multiply these tiny triumphs by a million, add them all together, and they are nothing—less than nothing, a positive impediment—measured against one draught of that living water Christ offers to the spiritually thirsty.[8]

God's Gift of Life

This was Jesus' message to the woman at the well. He told her that as long as she continued drinking from worldly troughs, she would always thirst again. But, He added, "whoever drinks of the water that I will give him will never be thirsty forever. The water that I will give him will become in him a spring of water welling up to eternal life" (John 4:14).

There is a *condition* attached to Jesus' offer. He said, "Whoever drinks. . . ." Jesus did not say that we must fulfill some quest or perform morally or religiously at a certain high level. He did not place a price tag on His living water. Instead, He simply said, "Whoever drinks. . . ." He was speaking, of course, of simple faith. John 3:16 tells us, "For God so loved the world, that he gave his only Son, that *whoever believes* in him should not perish but have eternal life" (emphasis added). Leon Morris says:

"The gift of the living water is not a reward for meritorious service. It is a gift that brings to anyone who receives it, no matter how insignificant and limited he or she may be, a totally new experience, a new power, a new life—the life that is eternal."[9]

Notice that this woman's sins did not keep Jesus from offering her salvation. He brought up her sins later in the conversation, not before but after He offered salvation, knowing that if she believed, His death on the cross would cleanse her from all sin. George Hutchinson writes, "Christ, who makes offer of grace before we seek it, will not refuse it to them who ask it, nor will former sins hinder their acceptance who come to seek grace; for even to this wicked woman he saith, 'Thou wouldest have asked, and he would have given thee living waters.'"[10]

When we fulfill the condition of salvation—receiving God's gift through faith alone—there is a glorious *consequence*. "Whoever drinks of the water that I will give him will never be thirsty forever." Jesus offers to satisfy our souls. This does not mean that all our trials cease and that life in this world is transformed into unending ease. Far from it! To follow Jesus is to pick up the cross and endure many hardships in life—not the least of which is our warfare with sin. But we gain soul fulfillment through our fellowship with God. Earthly things lose their appeal—the more worldly and sinful they are, the more thoroughly their luster fades—and we find permanent satisfaction for the thirst of our souls.

Lastly, Jesus spoke of a *change* that would result: "The water that I will give him will become in him a spring of water welling up to eternal life" (John 4:14b). These words refer to new life from the Holy Spirit. To be born again is to have a spiritual fountain welling up within you, as God Himself lives and moves in your heart.

The results of this change, with the ever-flowing fountain of spiritual power it opens up in us, are faith, godliness, and unfailing spiritual joy. Do you experience that? If you are not a Christian, this is what Jesus offers you—not the dreary, negative lifestyle you have been told that

Christians endure. If you come to Jesus, He will save you through faith and give you life abundant (see John 10:10).

If you are a Christian, are you experiencing this? Do you enjoy the blessings of the Holy Spirit's fountain in your heart? Ponce de Leon sought a Fountain of Youth that did not exist. Tragically, however, far too many Christians have found the true fountain of eternal, spiritual life but know little of its blessings of righteousness, peace, and joy. This is one reason our witness is often ineffective.

There are a number of explanations for this. Some Christians live close to the world and fill their hearts with worldly things. Are you like that? Are you still filling your soul with water that will leave you thirsty again? If so, wean your heart from earthly pleasures and start serving Jesus at home, in your work, and in your play. Stop craving for worldly success, stop drinking from worldly troughs, and renew your commitment to Christ, and you will find refreshing waters flowing freely once again. Other Christians have stopped up the spring of the Holy Spirit with sinful habits or attitudes. If you are truly a Christian, you can never ultimately block God's Spirit, but how much better for you to repent or forgive as needed and to walk in the light, cleansed by Christ's blood and refreshed by His fellowship. Jesus says to all who come to Him, for the first time or once again, "Whoever drinks of the water that I will give him will never be thirsty forever."

The Samaritan woman heard Jesus' offer of life—its condition, its consequence, and its change—and still responded with only worldly understanding. She said, "Sir, give me this water, so that I will not be thirsty or have to come here to draw water" (John 4:15). But Jesus was not done with her—He would continue working into her heart until she understood and believed. When she finally did, she responded with a joy that changed her life and the lives of many others. May we likewise know the gift of God and the Savior who offers it, and may many others drink from His living water through our witness in the world.

NOTES

1 Cited from *Our Country*, Vol. 1, accessed online at http://www.publicbookshelf. com/public_html/Our_Country_Vol_1/complete_text.txt, Ch. 6.

2 Ibid.

3 Ibid.

4 Joseph "Skip" Ryan, *That You May Believe* (Wheaton, Ill.: Crossway Books, 2003), 100.

5 Andreas J. Kostenberger, *John* (Grand Rapids, Mich.: Baker Books, 2004), 150.

6 St. Augustine, *The Confessions* (Oxford, England: Oxford University Press, 1991), 3.

7 Arthur W. Pink, *The Seven Sayings of the Saviour on the Cross* (Grand Rapids, Mich.: Baker Books, 1958), 96.

8 Cited in Bruce Milne, *The Message of John: Here Is Your King!* (Downers Grove, Ill.: InterVarsity Press, 1993), 84.

9 Leon Morris, *Reflections on the Gospel of John* (Peabody, Mass.: Hendrickson Publishers, 1986), 136.

10 George Hutchinson, *Exposition of the Gospel of John* (Lafayette, Ind.: Sovereign Grace Publishers, 2001), 60.

Questions for discussion and reflection:

1. Why did Ponce de Leon have such a great desire for the "Fountain of Youth"? How are many people like him today? What opportunities does this fact present for sharing the gospel?

2. The author claims that "Jesus Himself . . . is the fountain of eternal life." How would you explain this statement to a non-Christian?

3. Jesus was skillful at using situations to lead into a gospel presentation. Have you ever done the same? Can you think of relevant situations from life today that would serve as springboards for witnessing the gospel?

4. Why didn't the woman at the well understand Jesus' offer of "living water"? What makes it similarly difficult for people to understand Christian ideas today? How can we help them?

5. What is the relationship between physical thirst and spiritual thirst? How does Jesus' statement that "If anyone thirsts . . ." embolden your witness of the gospel?

6. What is the link between water and eternal life? How does Jesus use this metaphor to describe the gift of salvation and to encourage His followers to seek the fullness of the blessing He offers?

7. What was the true tragedy of Ponce de Leon and of those who seek satisfaction in the things of this world? How is this tragedy being lived out today by many people? What would you say to someone like Ponce?

8. How has the living water of Christ satisfied the thirst of your soul?

Chapter 11

DEALING WITH SIN

John 4:16–19

Jesus said to her, "Go, call your husband, and come here." The woman answered him, "I have no husband." Jesus said to her, "You are right in saying, 'I have no husband'; for you have had five husbands, and the one you now have is not your husband. What you have said is true."

—John 4:16–18

Every preacher knows that people do not like to hear about sin. People regard sin as a dreary, negative topic and prefer to think about more positive and comfortable themes. The situation is like that of a visitor to a leper colony, a comparison that is especially apt since the Bible uses leprosy as a picture of sin. The last thing lepers want to hear about is leprosy! They have to deal with it all the time, so they are not likely to gather in large numbers to hear someone speak about the nature and effects of leprosy. Since they are suffering, they prefer to listen to something entertaining to divert their minds!

So why should Christians dwell on sin? James Montgomery Boice answers: "It is simply because Christians are realists. They recognize that sin is an everyday experience and the number one problem of mankind. What is more, they recognize that the Bible everywhere insists upon this."[1]

However, Christians do not talk about sin simply as an exercise in realism, but because we have good news to bring. It is one thing to gather lepers to lecture on skin ailments. It is quite another to stand among those who are suffering and dying in order to proclaim the cure that will save them! Christians speak about sin because, in Jesus Christ, we have found and offer to others a cure for this all-pervasive plague.

God Knows Our Sin

It was for precisely this reason that Jesus brought the subject of sin into His conversation with the Samaritan woman. He had come through this region that other Jews avoided in order to meet with her. He had connected with her on a personal basis, then offered her God's gift of eternal life. Sitting with her at the well, Jesus said, "If you knew the gift of God, and who it is that is saying to you, 'Give me a drink,' you would have asked him and he would have given you living water" (John 4:10). The woman does not seem to have grasped His real meaning right away, but she was impressed enough to ask for the living water He offered: "Sir, give me this water, so that I will not be thirsty or have to come here to draw water" (John 4:15). That was an imperfect request, but a request all the same, so Jesus took the next step in offering her salvation by bringing up the problem of her sin. "Jesus said to her, 'Go, call your husband, and come here.' The woman answered him, 'I have no husband.' Jesus said to her, 'You are right in saying, "I have no husband"; for you have had five husbands, and the one you now have is not your husband. What you have said is true'" (John 4:16–18).

It is remarkable that Jesus was able to say this, because it seems that He had never met this woman before. Jesus was not from her district, so there is no reason to think that He knew her by reputation. The fact that she came to draw water in the heat of the "sixth hour" (John 4:6), that is, noon, suggests that other women did not welcome her company, perhaps because of her morals. But a hint like that would not have provided the specific information Jesus had. How did Jesus know that this woman had had five husbands—the implication is that this touched the main sin area in her life—and was currently living with a man who was not her husband?

The only reasonable explanation is that Jesus possessed superhuman abilities because of His divine nature. This has been John's emphasis from the start of his Gospel. Referring to Jesus as "the Word," the Gospel's first verse says, "The Word was with God, and the Word was God." Throughout his Gospel, John refers to Jesus as the "Son of God." The first half of John's Gospel is often called "the Book of Signs" because it is organized around miracles that show Jesus' deity: the transforming of water into wine, the healing of the ruler's son, the walking on water, the healing of the lame man by the pool, the feeding of the five thousand, the restoring of the blind man's sight, and the raising of Lazarus from the tomb. John ends his book by telling us, "These [accounts of Jesus' ministry] are written so that you may believe that Jesus is the Christ, the Son of God, and that by believing you may have life in his name" (John 20:31). Jesus' divinity, then, is the reason He could recite details from the life of a woman He had just met. Just as the weariness and thirst that brought Jesus to this well displayed His full humanity, His omniscient knowledge of the woman's life history displayed His full deity.

Jesus' detailed knowledge of this woman's past also proves a point more pertinent to us, namely, that God has full knowledge of our sin. To sin is to violate God's law, and God, who sees all things, knows when we break His law. Arthur W. Pink explains how this can be:

> God is omniscient. He knows everything. . . . He is perfectly acquainted with every detail in the life of every being in heaven, in earth, in hell. "He knoweth what is in the darkness" (Dan. 2:22). Nothing escapes His notice, nothing can be hidden from Him. . . . His knowledge is perfect. He never errs, never changes, never overlooks anything. "Neither is there any creature that is not manifest in His sight: but all things are naked and opened unto the eyes of Him with whom we have to do" (Heb. 4:13).[2]

The Bible gives abundant testimony to God's knowledge of our sin. Cain killed his brother in secret, but God saw it and held him to account. Sarah laughed in the silence of her tent, but God heard her. Achan hid the wedge of gold he stole from fallen Jericho, but God brought his theft to light. Jonah hid his rebellion in the deep hold of a ship bound for Tarshish, but God marked the ship with a precisely targeted storm. God rebuked the very thoughts of His hardened people, saying to Israel, "I know the things that come into your mind" (Ezek. 11:5).

An incident from the life of King David provides perhaps the starkest evidence that God knows our most secret sins. Second Samuel 11 records David's adultery with Bathsheba, along with the cover-up in which he employed all his cunning and royal power. David tied up all the loose ends, arranging even the murder of Bathsheba's potentially suspicious husband. But the chapter ends with these words: "The thing that David had done displeased the LORD" (2 Sam. 11:27). How did God know? The psalmist answers, "You have set our iniquities before you, our secret sins in the light of your presence" (Ps. 90:8).

It is true, of course, that the God who sees all things is a loving and gracious God, a kind and merciful Father to His children. But He is also a holy God. Paul writes to Christians, "Do not be deceived: God is not mocked, for whatever one sows, that will he also reap" (Gal. 6:7). There can be little doubt that many of us experience difficulties because of our sins. That is true not merely because of the natural consequences of sin, but because God chastens us, so that many of our hardships are sent by God in direct response to our sins. Hebrews 12:6 says, "The Lord disciplines the one he loves, and chastises every son whom he receives." So even those whose sins have been forgiven through the blood of Christ nonetheless suffer in this life because of their sins. If we want God's kindness toward us to have a free reign, we will not present God with sins that require Him to discipline us. The path of obedience is ever the path of blessing.

However uncomfortable it makes us feel, it is healthy for us to realize that our every moment is lived before the face of God. Knowing this will rescue us from the folly of thinking that sin can be cultivated unawares. We are all more tempted to sin when we think no one will ever know. Therefore, the knowledge that our every deed is recorded in heaven should preserve us from temptation and stiffen our resolve to live in obedience to God's law.

Knowledge of our sin has other benefits. It helps cultivate a right humility. The apostle Paul's spiritual progress was paralleled by an increasing awareness of his sin. In one of his earliest letters, he describes himself as "the least of the apostles" (1 Cor. 15:9). A little later, he calls himself "the very least of all the saints" (Eph. 3:8). By the end of his ministry, he says, "Christ Jesus came into the world to save sinners, of whom I am the foremost" (1 Tim. 1:15). Our spiritual maturation will likewise progress as we see more clearly the true depth of our sin, the true holiness of God, and the great gulf between us—and thus also see the true greatness of His love for us that moved Him to give His Son to save sinners so infinitely below Him. This is why the humblest Christians are the happiest Christians, and why humble and happy Christians tend to be holy Christians, as well. All of these benefits stem from an awareness of our sin.

Our Sin Separates Us from God

As we have studied Jesus' meeting with the Samaritan woman, we have been taking notes on His evangelistic example. Jesus shows us here that in order to win a soul to God, we have to deal with sin. The reason is that *our sin separates us from God.* This fact is lost on many Christians today, who have observed that sinners do not like to hear about sin. Knowing that to bring up sin is to have fewer people attending your church or buying your books, evangelical leaders increasingly avoid the topic. But Jesus' example shows the folly of this trend. While it is true that we achieve a greater popularity by neglecting to mention sin, we cannot actually bring people to God without confronting this deadly problem.

There are many ways in which sin separates us from God, but I want to focus on three. These are all reasons why sin needs to be addressed and dealt with.

First, sin separates us from God because *it offends and repels God's holy nature.* A friend told me about his mother, who loved her cat but was disgusted by rodents. So when her cat tried to enter the door with a mouse in its teeth, she would greet the cat with a broom, refusing to let it into the house. God is that way with regard to sin: He will not let it into His holy heaven.

This reminds us that God's law is not an arbitrary list of do's and don'ts. Rather, the Ten Commandments inform us of things that are hateful to God. He is the true God, so He hates idolatry. He is love, so He hates murder. He is pure, so He hates adultery. God is true, so He hates lying. Therefore, to stand before God in your sin is to be subject to His wrath. Paul says, "For the wrath of God is revealed from heaven against all ungodliness and unrighteousness of men" (Rom. 1:18a).

That leads to the second way in which sin separates us from God: *It brings us under His judgment.* God is a righteous judge who must condemn sinners. Abraham asked, "Shall not the Judge of all the earth do what is just?" (Gen. 18:25). The answer is yes! God must do what is just; this means that He must judge all sin.

Some argue that this was true only of the Old Testament God, and that now that Jesus has come, we have a nicer God who is more easygoing about sin. But that is untrue; God has not changed since Abraham's day, when He destroyed Sodom and Gomorrah. If anything, the New Testament's warnings about God's judgment on all sin are worse than those in the Old Testament. Jesus Himself said: "Do not fear those who kill the body but cannot kill the soul. Rather fear him who can destroy both soul and body in hell" (Matt. 10:28). The last New Testament book, Revelation, depicts God's future day of judgment, saying, "I saw the dead, great and small, standing before the throne, and books were opened. . . . And the dead were judged by what was written in the books, according to what they had done" (Rev. 20:12).

Many people don't think of themselves as sinners worthy of judgment. But if you commit just three sins per day—if you are irreverent, dishonest, malicious, lustful, or covetous just three times in a day—and the great majority of us break God's law in thought or deed at least that many times in a hour!—you will commit more than a thousand sins per year. If you live for seventy-five years, as many of us will, when you die you will arrive in God's court with seventy-five thousand sins to be dealt with. How would a human judge respond to a criminal with seventy-five thousand violations of the civil law? Surely he would impose the maximum penalty! God hates sin more than any human judge, and He has decreed that the "wages of sin is death" (Rom. 6:23). How important it is, then, that we find a way to deal with our sin before appearing before God's judgment.

Third, sin separates us from God because *it makes us uneasy in His presence.* Sin not only keeps God from us, it keeps us from God. After Adam and Eve sinned, they first tried to cover themselves with fig leaves and then fled from God altogether (Gen. 3:7–8). When Jesus miraculously filled Peter's nets to bursting with fish, Peter realized he was in the presence of God. Falling before Jesus, he cried, "Depart from me, for I am a sinful man, O Lord" (Luke 5:8). Chastened by his sin, even Peter did not feel comfortable near Jesus.

Jesus had invited the Samaritan woman to ask for God's gift of salvation. She did ask, however imperfectly. So Jesus immediately confronted her with her sin, because conviction of sin is a necessary step in receiving the gospel. The bad news must come first in order for the good news to make sense and appeal to our hearts. D. Martyn Lloyd-Jones writes:

A gospel which merely says "Come to Jesus", and offers Him as a Friend, and offers a marvellous new life, without convicting of sin, is not New Testament evangelism. The essence of evangelism is to start by preaching the law; and it is because the law has not been preached that we have had so much superficial evangelism. . . . This means that we must explain that mankind is confronted by the holiness of God, by His demands, and also by the consequences of sin.[3]

Loving Christians seek to convict others of sin because Jesus Christ is the Savior of sinners. Paul writes, "While we were still weak, at the right time Christ died for the ungodly. . . . God shows his love for us in that while we were still sinners, Christ died for us" (Rom. 5:6–8). This means not only that sinners may be saved by Jesus, but that only sinners may be saved by Jesus. If you will not admit yourself to be a sinner, worthy of God's fiery judgment, then Jesus and His blood are of no use to you. You will have to find another way to be justified before God, and even ten thousand times ten thousand years in hell will not be enough to pay your debt. We must admit the bad news to hear the good news; we must be sinners to be saved. Pink says: "We have to be abased before we can be exalted. We have to be stript of the filthy rags of our self-righteousness before we are ready for the garments of salvation. We have to come to God as beggars, empty-handed, before we can receive the gift of eternal life."[4]

Jesus Came to Deal with Our Sin

Jesus confronted this woman with her sin because He loved her, because He knew her sin, and because her sin stood between her and God. How fitting it is that Jesus spoke to her about her sin, and that He was the One to set this example for us, because Jesus came into the world to deal with the problem of our sin.

From start to finish, Jesus' life and ministry were aimed at dealing with our sin. The angel who announced His birth told Joseph, "You shall call his name Jesus, for he will save his people from their sins" (Matt. 1:21b). This is why Jesus was born into obscure poverty, His infant body placed not on a royal bed but in an animal's feeding trough. Though very God of very God, He was born into humiliation so as to take up the cause of sinners. This is why Jesus insisted on receiving the baptism of repentance. John the Baptist tried to refuse, saying, "'I need to be baptized by you, and do you come to me?' But Jesus answered him, 'Let it be so now, for thus it is fitting for us to fulfill all righteousness.' Then he consented" (Matt. 3:14b–15). This is why Jesus associated with sinners, a practice that drew the criticism of the Pharisees. They complained to His disciples: "'Why does your teacher eat with tax collectors and sinners?' But when [Jesus] heard it, he said, 'Those who are well have no need of a physician, but those who are sick. . . . I came not to call the righteous, but sinners'" (Matt. 9:11b–13).

Above all, this is why Jesus meekly submitted when He was unjustly convicted, even though Pontius Pilate had declared Him completely innocent. This was why Jesus accepted the dreadful lash of the Roman scourge, when He might have called down legions of angels to His defense. This is why He permitted Himself to be abused, allowed His body to be draped with a mock purple robe, and submitted His head to be pierced with a bloody crown of thorns—that He might be presented before history as the very picture of sinful mankind judged, condemned, and punished. And this is why the Son of God willingly took up the cross, forsaken by God and man, and died for sins He did not commit. Jesus Himself summed up the purpose of His whole saving work: "The Son of Man came not to be served but to serve, and to give his life as a ransom for many" (Matt. 20:28).

Do you see why, therefore, we not only *can* but *must* bring up the issue of sin in our offer of God's salvation? If sin was so important to God that He sent His only beloved Son into the world to deal specifically with it; if sin is so great a barrier between God and man that only the precious blood of Christ could remove it; and if Jesus was so committed to the salvation of sinners that He was willing to go to this horrific length to achieve it, how dare we cover up the topic of sin as some embarrassment to us or an impediment to the success of Christ's church! Do you see why we must be willing to ask people to confess their sins in worship that is offered up in Christ's name? Do you see why we must preach a gospel not just of cheery sentimentality but of the true and bad news of sin for which Christ paid so great a cost?

But notice, too, the care with which Jesus handled the matter of sin with this woman. Many would glare at her and denounce her for sin. But Jesus coyly told her, "Go, call your husband, and come here" (John 4:16). He knew what she was going to say, and she said it: "I have no husband" (John 4:17a). Jesus wanted the confession to come from her lips. When it came, He drove home the point: "You are right in saying, 'I have no husband'; for you have had five husbands, and the one you now have is not your husband. What you have said is true" (John 4:17b–18). It is unreasonable for us to expect to match Jesus' skill, since we lack His perfect knowledge and grace. But His example shows us that we should exercise care in bringing people to conviction of sin—as Nathan did when he confronted King David for his sin with Bathsheba—and that we should seek the Holy Spirit's help through prayer both for our own conduct and for the response of the one whom we hope to bring to conviction of sin and faith in Christ.

While there are many ways to bring others to conviction, there is only one way for us to respond when confronted with our own sin. We must allow God's law to slay us so that Christ's gospel will bring us to life. We must confess our sin, repent, and believe on Jesus. This is true both for those coming to Christ for the first time and for veteran Christians who are faced with their sins. The Christian is not one who has never sinned or never does sin. Rather, the true Christian is the one who is quick to confess his or her sin, who then appeals to the shed blood of Jesus for cleansing and forgiveness, and who follows through on that repentance with a fresh resolve to walk in true faith and holiness by the power of God's Holy Spirit.

The Samaritan woman was not yet ready to do that. She responded to Jesus in the way so many others have and do. She tried to change the subject: "The woman said to him, 'Sir, I perceive that you are a prophet'" (John 4:19). She did not and could not deal with her sin because she had not yet recognized who Jesus was. Do you? Jesus is the

One who enables us to face and deal with our sin, so as to be forgiven and set free. The Bible presents Jesus as the Lamb of God who bore our sin before God's wrath, the Substitute who took our place in judgment, and the Redeemer who purchased our freedom with His blood. If you see Jesus as the true Savior that He is, then there is no reason for you not to deal with your sin: confessing it, condemning it, and bringing it to the cross. There your sin will be taken away and your heart will be set free—from condemnation to life, from bondage to holy freedom—as the gift of God in Jesus Christ.

Jesus wasn't discouraged by the Samaritan woman's unwillingness to face her sin. So neither should we be discouraged when this happens. People are likely to attempt to divert us from the chief issues of salvation. But we should do what Jesus did, which was to direct her questions back to Himself, as we will see in the next chapter. Every question, every evasion, and every objection can be made to lead to Jesus. But let us not shy away from the vital matter of sin, being always ready to direct our witness to the Savior of sinners, whose gospel we are privileged to share.

NOTES

[1] James Montgomery Boice, *The Gospel of John,* 5 vols. (Grand Rapids, Mich.: Baker Books, 1999), 1:284–285.

[2] Arthur W. Pink, *The Attributes of God* (Grand Rapids, Mich.: Baker Books, 1975), 18.

[3] D. Martyn Lloyd-Jones, *Expositions on the Sermon on the Mount,* 2 vols. (Grand Rapids, Mich.: Eerdmans Publishing, 1959), 1:235.

[4] Arthur W. Pink, *The Seven Sayings of the Saviour on the Cross* (Grand Rapids, Mich.: Baker Books, 1958), 31.

Questions for discussion and reflection:

1. In your experience, how do people respond to a discussion of sin? Why do people respond in this way? If people are turned off by sin, should we avoid the subject in our witness to the gospel? If not, why not?

2. Jesus had the advantage of a divine perspective on sin. How do we tend to view sin differently than God does? How does a casual attitude toward sin affect our lives?

3. How do you feel about God's minute knowledge of your sin? Does it make you feel uneasy? Why? How *should* we react?

4. The author states that a deeper knowledge of our sin brings great blessing to our lives. Have you experienced this? How can a deeper sense of sin lead to greater humility and joy?

5. How does sin affect our relationship with God? How does sin affect God's relationship with us?

6. How does the Bible's teaching on sin lead to good news for those who believe in Jesus?

7. What are some ways in which we can handle the topic of sin in a careful and sensitive way? Have you made mistakes in this regard that you want to avoid in the future? Have you had some positive experiences?

8. Pray for one another, that sin would not hinder your relationship with God and your usefulness as an evangelist.

Chapter 12

THE CRY
OF NEW LIFE

John 4:27–30

> So the woman left her water jar and went away into town
> and said to the people, "Come, see a man who told me all
> that I ever did. Can this be the Christ?"   —*John 4:28–29*

S easoned evangelists will tell you that it is very hard to get a
response from an unbelieving heart. The reason is that many
people work strenuously to avoid facing their sin. An outstanding example is the Samaritan woman in her response to Jesus' offer of
salvation.

When Jesus revealed His detailed knowledge of her sinful life, she
said, "Sir, I perceive that you are a prophet" (John 4:19). She would
have been wise to entreat Jesus for salvation and embrace His offer of
living water. But instead—and how typical this is of rebellious hearts—
she attempted to divert the conversation. Raising the issue of a local
controversy regarding worship, she said, "Our fathers worshiped on
this mountain, but you say that in Jerusalem is the place where people
ought to worship" (John 4:20). When Jesus answered this question, she
attempted to wriggle out by another way—by appealing to the supposed
limitations of the Bible. She said, "I know that Messiah is coming (he

who is called Christ). When he comes, he will tell us all things" (John 4:25). Of course, she didn't really want to know about the Messiah—the point was to end this annoying conversation dealing with her sin!

What is the Christian to do to help someone determined not to consider the claims of Christ? On numerous occasions like this, I have simply pressed a Bible into such a person's hands, saying: "Why don't I give you a copy of God's Word to read for yourself. If you are really interested—and I hope you are—you will find the truth about Jesus in here." Often, I have advised people to start by reading the Gospel of John, and in some cases I have learned that a man or woman read it and came to believe the gospel.

Jesus, however, had certain advantages over the rest of us when it comes to evangelism. I can only give the Word to a reluctant believer, but Jesus *is* the Word. I can only say, "Jesus is the Messiah." But when the Samaritan woman mused that things would get sorted out someday when the Messiah finally came, Jesus was able to respond, "I who speak to you am he" (John 4:26).

There is no greater witness to the gospel than Jesus Himself, which is why the ultimate goal of our evangelism is to bring people to meet with Him. It is always marvelous when someone comes to realize the truth about our Lord, but imagine what it must have been like as the Lord Jesus revealed His divine person to this woman, with the evident effect that her eyes were opened to see that He was the Messiah of whom she had spoken. Did her eyes bulge? Did tears flow down her face? Did she kneel before Him and grasp His hands? We do not know, but as we will see in this chapter, it is evident that her unbelief was overwhelmed by Jesus' self-revelation and that her life was changed forever by what happened in that moment.

The Samaritan woman is the first person in the Gospel of John to be clearly born again. She had come to the well a worldly woman, ignorant of saving truth and thinking only of her material need for water. But she went back to her village transformed, with truth and life to share. What made the change? She had met Jesus and had seen His divine glory. The result was living water welling up in her heart unto eternal life.

But the Samaritan woman's heart was not the only one that needed to be taught by Jesus on that day. John tells us that while her dramatic transformation was taking place, Jesus' disciples returned from Sychar, where they had gone to buy food while He rested by the well. They missed His instructive dialogue with the Samaritan woman, but they returned in time for the glorious finale of the woman's conversion. John tells us: "Just then his disciples came back. They marveled that he was talking with a woman, but no one said, 'What do you seek?' or, 'Why are you talking with her?'" (John 4:27).

The disciples thought only in terms of the stifling social conventions of their time and could not see the spiritual transformation taking place. They could not imagine a sinner becoming a saint, and they were especially skeptical about a Gentile being admitted into the company of God's people. They were surprised by grace—indeed, *dismayed* or *appalled* by grace might be more accurate! Their minds were fixed on the social status quo rather than the ground-shaking effects of Christ's coming. John, who was present as one of these unspiritual disciples, tells us that they wanted to challenge Jesus, saying, "Why are you talking with her?" That is the way false and dead religion always responds to grace. Had they asked, Jesus' answer would have been, "To give her living water." But the disciples' mouths were stopped—whether by astonishment or by God Himself we are not told—so that they were not permitted to desecrate the holy occasion.

This portion of the story raises an important question for those who are sincere in wanting to lead souls to salvation in Christ: How do we know that a person has really been saved? The disciples were dubious about the conversion of this Samaritan woman. So how can we have confidence that she was truly born again—and that others like her today have found new life in Christ?

When we studied Jesus' teaching on this topic in John 3, we saw that the new birth is known only by its effects. Jesus said, "The wind blows where it wishes, and you hear its sound, but you do not know where it comes from or where it goes. So it is with everyone who is born of the Spirit" (John 3:8). Just as wind is seen by its effects, the new birth has necessary consequences that always occur and by which we may know that we or others truly are saved. John's narrative highlights three signs of true salvation. It is essential for those seeking to lead others to Christ to know these evidences.

Confession of Faith in Christ

When a doctor delivers a baby, the first thing he wants to hear is the baby's cry. This tells him that air has entered the baby's lungs and that the child has started to breathe. So it is with the spiritual rebirth. When the Spirit enters the heart, the new life He brings causes the spiritual infant to cry out, confessing his or her faith in Jesus Christ. This is the first clear sign that true salvation has occurred.

This is a matter of some confusion to people. Many believe that the new birth is *caused* by a profession of faith, but the situation is exactly reversed: A confession of faith in Christ is a *result* of a person being born again of the Holy Spirit. Jesus taught, "Unless one is born again he cannot see the kingdom of God" (John 3:3). But that does not make a public confession of faith optional. James Montgomery Boice comments: "Some persons think that they can be secret believers, but the Word of God never considers this a possibility. What does the Word of God say? 'Whoever acknowledges me before men, I will also acknowledge him before my Father in heaven. But whoever disowns me before men, I will disown him before my Father in heaven' (Mt. 10:32–33)."[1]

Here is where we see the main difference between Nicodemus, to whom Jesus witnessed in John 3, and the woman by the well in John 4. Nicodemus was a much more religious and moral person, but he left Jesus without professing his faith. It is my belief that Nicodemus struggled with this until he actually saw Jesus dying on the cross, after which he finally confessed his faith by going with Joseph of Arimathea to bury

Jesus' body (John 19:39). But the woman at the well, having beheld Jesus' deity when He revealed Himself as the Messiah, responded with a public confession of faith that clearly showed her new birth. John 4:28–29 tells us, "The woman left her water jar and went away into town and said to the people, 'Come, see a man who told me all that I ever did. Can this be the Christ?'" From her subsequent conduct, it is evident that she was saying, "I have found the Messiah," and her public confession to her neighbors demonstrated her rebirth.

Change in Life

The second sign that the Samaritan woman had been saved was the change that occurred in her life. According to the Bible, a bare confession of faith is not in itself enough to demonstrate a new birth. The reason is that a confession of faith is not credible unless it is accompanied by a changed life. It is one thing to recite "the sinner's prayer" or give verbal assent to the gospel, but a true conversion will lead to a living faith—not a dead faith—that bears the spiritual fruit of change in one's life.

One of the great illustrations of this is the life of John Newton. He was born into a Christian home, but Newton's parents died when he was only 6, and he was sent to live with an unbelieving relative. Christianity was mocked in that home, and he was abused and neglected. So Newton ran away to be a sailor and fell into gross sin. After a while, he deserted to live in one of the worst areas of Africa because, as he recounts, he could "sin his full" there.

Newton joined a slave trader, who mistreated him so badly that he ran away again and joined the crew of a slave ship. Since Newton was a trained navigator, he soon became the ship's mate. One day, however, he broke into the ship's rum supply and got so drunk he fell overboard; he was saved only when one of the crew members harpooned him in the thigh and hauled him back in.

As the ship was nearing its port in Scotland, it entered a storm and began to sink. Newton was sent down into the pitch blackness of the hold to work the pump with the slaves. For days on end he pumped, and in the darkness he recalled the Bible verses his mother had taught him as a little child. They spoke of God's grace and the cross where the Savior had died for his forgiveness. Through God's Word, he was born again and cried out in saving faith. How do we know? Because when the storm passed and the ship arrived safely home, Newton left the ship, sought out a church, and began a new life that was increasingly godly. He went on to be greatly used of God as a notable preacher and great writer of hymns, a trophy of God's amazing grace, as revealed by both his confession of faith and his changed life.

What about the Samaritan woman? What evidence do we have that she began a new life when she believed on Jesus? John indicates this in beautiful fashion, I believe, by telling us, "The woman left her water jar and went away into town" (John 4:28). This detail reminds us that John was an eyewitness to these events; only someone who was personally present could record a detail like this.

But what could John be suggesting by telling us that the woman left her water jar behind? We should note that John uses the imagery of water throughout his Gospel. Jesus performed His first miracle by turning water into wine. The water jars at the wedding in Cana were used for ceremonial washing under the old covenant law. The same word is used here for the Samaritan woman's water jar; it was not a small container, but likely a substantial clay vessel that she would carry with great effort on her head or hip. In chapter 5, John again brings water into his Gospel. There, Jesus healed a lame man who had been hoping to be cured by the waters of the pool of Bethesda. In all of these instances, sitting water—like that in Jacob's well—depicts powerless, outward religion, which Jesus replaces with the living water of true spiritual power and life.

This trend in John's Gospel suggests that by leaving the water jar, the Samaritan woman was leaving behind a lifeless religion of ceremonies and works. F. F. Bruce argues, "Her abandonment of the waterpot is a parable of the renunciation of the old ceremonial law, practiced by Jews and Samaritans alike, on the part of those who through faith in Christ have received the divine gift of eternal life."[2] She had brought that jar to Jacob's well to draw its stagnant water, but she had found there living water instead. Jesus had offered it to her: "If you knew the gift of God . . . you would have asked him, and he would have given you living water. . . . The water that I will give . . . will become . . . a spring of water welling up to eternal life" (John 4:10–14).

The water jar also signified the overall emptiness of the woman's life. J. C. Ryle says: "Grace once introduced into the heart drives out old tastes and interests. A converted person no longer cares for what he once cared for. A new tenant is in the house: a new pilot is at the helm. The whole world looks different."[3] This is how God's grace changes us. The woman experienced the expulsive power of a new affection: thoughts of Jesus drove out her former desires and filled her with a zeal to declare His glory.

If there has been no similar change in your life, then your confession of faith in Christ is doubtful at best. Boice comments:

> I wonder if you have experienced a change in your life and values as a result of pondering the truths of the gospel. I do not mean, "Have you been totally transformed overnight?" That does not often happen, although it can. Generally, the Christian life is one of growth, just as a baby must grow through childhood, adolescence, and into adult life. . . . [But] has there been at least a partial transformation of your values? Are you different now since you have believed? Are you being changed?[4]

Again, the woman's water jar is instructive about the struggle many people experience. They are held back by remnants of their former lives that they have not given up for Jesus—some false source of comfort, some sinful habit, or some ungodly ambition they have failed to renounce. These remnants keep them from the kind of lifestyle change that would give them the joy and assurance of salvation they ought to have.

A helpful book in understanding the new birth was written by a little-known pastor in early nineteenth-century Brooklyn named Ichabod Spencer. In *A Pastor's Sketches*, he depicts his many one-on-one encounters in leading people to faith, one of which involved a man who literally needed to give up a container like the Samaritan woman's. A middle-aged farmer had been attending church faithfully for many years. His wife was a vibrant Christian, but he never showed any personal response. At the wife's invitation, Spencer dropped by their home to speak to the man about his soul. The farmer admitted that though he attended church, he never felt the love of God or any spiritual power, and as a result he lived a gloomy, fearful existence. Spencer assured him that God had opened the way to salvation if only he would yield himself to Jesus as Savior and Lord. The man offered to try, but over the course of some months, nothing happened.

One day, Spencer happened upon the farmer bringing his wagon into town. As they talked, Spencer spied a brown jug under the farmer's seat—a vessel not unlike the one the Samaritan woman brought to Jacob's well. He gently inquired about the jug's contents, learning that it was filled with rum. Further inquiry revealed that the man was not a drunkard, but whenever he was low in spirits or troubled at night, he would minister to himself with rum. Spencer immediately realized the situation: When the Holy Spirit was pressing on the farmer's heart to lead him to Christ, he was spiritually dulling himself with the rum. The problem was not alcohol as such, but a worldly source of relief that was standing in the way of repentance and faith in Christ.

Spencer told the farmer this and urgently called him to renounce his fleshly compulsion. There was a large rock beside the wagon and, Spencer recalled, "His eye fixed upon it, and then glanced back to the jug upon his knee. Then he looked at the rock, and then at his jug again, and then at me. And thus his eye continued to wander from one to another of these three objects, as if it could not get beyond them. . . . Finally he seized the poor jug by its side, wrapping the long fingers of his right hand half round it, and slowly rising from his seat, he stretched up his tall frame to its full length, and lifting the brown jug aloft . . . he hurled it, with all his might, against the rock, dashing it into a thousand pieces." Spencer tells us that "within a single month . . . that man became, as he believed, a child of God. His gloom and fears were gone, and he had peace, by faith in Jesus Christ."[5]

That is what you must do with whatever water jar or brown jug is holding you back from a saving embrace of Jesus Christ. Do not let any worldly concern keep you from the salvation life that Jesus has to give.

Concern for the Lost

The third sign that this woman was truly born again was her immediate concern for the spiritual well-being of others: "So the woman left her water jar and went away into town and said to the people, 'Come, see a man who told me all that I ever did. Can this be the Christ?'" (John 4:28–29). This part of the woman's story depicts what is true of us all, namely, that the day of her conversion to Christ was also the day of her appointment as an evangelist.

The Bible tells us that different believers receive different spiritual gifts. Some are gifted with expertise at teaching, others with a talent for encouragement, others with abilities in administration. But witnessing the gospel is not simply a spiritual gift given only to some. Rather, it is a duty every believer shares. More than that, it is the inevitable result of the overflow of the living water Jesus gives to all who believe. John Calvin said: "It is the nature of faith that we want to bring others to share eternal life with us when we have become partakers of it. The knowledge of God cannot lie buried and inactive in our hearts and not be made known to men."[6]

We saw earlier that John Newton was an example of a man whose confession of faith was confirmed by his changed life. But he also displayed a great concern for the lost. His greatest contribution was the hymn "Amazing Grace," in which he recounted for millions the basic facts of his conversion, and the salvation they, too, could receive:

Amazing Grace, how sweet the sound, that saved a wretch like me
I once was lost but now am found; was blind, but now I see.

This was also the testimony of the Samaritan woman. Her zeal to share her knowledge of Christ with the people of Sychar is particularly lovely when we remember that she seems to have been shunned by them previously. The best explanation for her appearance at the well in the heat of the day is that the other women did not approve of such a sinner's company at the normal time for drawing water, the early morning. The natural result of such rejection is resentment. Moreover, we might think that with her newfound faith the woman would want to remain close to Jesus. But even that proper response was overwhelmed by her burden for others to learn what she had discovered: that the Messiah had brought salvation to their corner of the world. Later, she would spend time with Jesus, for John tells us that He stayed in Sychar for two full days (John 4:43). But the new birth had already instilled in her a love for others she had not previously known. It was the love of God that Jesus had shown to her. This is the final proof of her new birth: first, she confessed her faith in Christ; second, she gave evidence of a changed life; and, third, she showed concern for the salvation of others by telling them about Jesus. The same marks will be evident in at least some measure in the lives of all who are born again to faith in Jesus Christ.

"Come!"

In conclusion, we should think about the words the Samaritan woman spoke to her fellow villagers: "Come, see a man who told me all that I ever did. Can this be the Christ?" (John 4:29). She had not yet advanced far in her understanding, but that did not stop her from giving a witness to Christ, and such a lack of deep understanding should not stop any of us from doing the same. Instead of being hindered by what she did not know, the Samaritan woman witnessed what she did know: the man she had met at the well was a true prophet and, what is more, He had revealed Himself as the long-awaited Messiah. This was enough—in addition to the obvious change in her life—to bring people out to see for themselves. As a result of her witness to the people of Sychar, "They went out of the town and were coming to him" (John 4:30). This is a fitting goal of our witness—simply to bring people to Jesus.

"Come" is the great invitation of the Christian gospel. It is what Jesus had said to the woman earlier in their conversation: "Jesus said to her, 'Go, call your husband, and come here'" (John 4:16). She then passed on this invitation to others. Boice exclaims: "Come! This is a great word of the Christian gospel. It has brought peace to millions of restless hearts and satisfaction to many that were empty and lonely."[7]

So many great verses of the Bible contain the invitation "Come!" This was God's call to Abraham to enter the Promised Land: "Come into the land which I shall show thee" (Acts 7:3, KJV). The angels spoke thus to the fearful women at the empty tomb: "Come, see the place where he lay" (Matt. 28:6). Jesus invited a would-be disciple, "Come, follow me" (Mark 10:21). He says to all, "Come to me, all who labor and are heavy laden, and I will give you rest" (Matt. 11:28). In the concluding words of the entire Bible, the Spirit joins His voice to the church for a joint witness to the world: "The Spirit and the Bride say, 'Come.' And let the one who hears say, 'Come.' And let the one who is thirsty come; let the one who desires take the water of life without price" (Rev. 22:17).

Understand, then, if you are one of those who do not enter into heaven but instead fall under the judgment of God, it will not be because no invitation was offered to you. God sent His only Son to bear the penalty of sin and to say to you, "Come!" If you will not come, you will perish in your sins to an eternity of wrath in which no offer of salvation will ever be heard again. But to answer Christ's call is to be renewed with eternal life and to inherit an eternity of glory. Won't you come? And if you have come, submit your lives to Jesus to be changed by Him and to be made a witness who extends His invitation to others, so that they, too, might come and be saved.

NOTES

[1] James Montgomery Boice, *The Gospel of John*, 5 vols. (Grand Rapids, Mich.: Baker Books, 1999), 1:308.

[2] F. F. Bruce, *The Gospel of John* (Grand Rapids, Mich.: Eerdmans Publishing, 1983), 112.

[3] J. C. Ryle, *Expository Thoughts on the Gospels: John*, 3 vols. (Edinburgh, Scotland, and Carlisle, Pa.: Banner of Truth Trust, 1999), 1:231.

[4] Boice, *The Gospel of John*, 1:309.

[5] Ichabod Spencer, *A Pastor's Sketches*, 2 vols. (Vestavia Hills, Ala.: Solid Ground Christian Books, 2001), 1:256–263.

[6] John Calvin, *New Testament Commentaries*, trans. T. H. L. Parker, 12 vols. (Grand Rapids, Mich.: Eerdmans Publishing, 1959), 4:104.

[7] Boice, *The Gospel of John*, 1:311.

Questions for discussion and reflection:

1. The Samaritan woman did her best to deflect Jesus' witness of the gospel. Have you experienced this? What are some ways you have tried to keep people focused in your witness? How should you respond when people bring up controversies and secondary matters during your witness?

2. Jesus concluded His witness to the Samaritan woman by revealing Himself as the Messiah. If our ultimate goal in witnessing is to reveal Jesus, how do we get people to see Him?

3. The author describes Jesus' disciples as "dismayed or appalled" by His witness to the Samaritan woman. Have you met Christians who acted similarly? Why did they act this way? How can you avoid having this attitude?

4. What response are we seeking from those who hear our witness? What elements make up a credible confession of faith in Jesus? Have you had the privilege of hearing people express their new-born faith in Christ? How did they do it?

5. Why is a bare confession of faith insufficient as a sign of the new birth? How does the Bible describe the relationship of faith to works?

6. Is it possible for us to accurately explain Christianity without noting the "water jars" that believers need to leave behind? What water jars have you left behind to follow Jesus? What kinds of things might others find themselves needing to leave behind in order to be Christians?

7. How does Christian faith provide us with a concern for the lost? In what ways have you experienced this? How has this experience changed your manner of life?

8. Consider the Bible passages that include the invitation "Come." Which do you find most lovely or compelling? How might you include these in your witness of the gospel?

Chapter 13

THE SAVIOR
OF THE WORLD

John 4:27–42

They said to the woman, "It is no longer because of what
you said that we believe, for we have heard for ourselves,
and we know that this is indeed the Savior of the world."

—*John 4:42*

Our studies have shown the importance of the theme of witness
in John's Gospel. We encountered this emphasis numerous
times in the first few chapters. The prologue highlights John
the Baptist: "He came as a witness, to bear witness about the light"
(John 1:7a). Later in chapter 1, we hear John's testimony: "Behold, the
Lamb of God, who takes away the sin of the world! . . . I have seen and
have borne witness that this is the Son of God" (John 1:29–34). This is
followed by the witness of Andrew, who told his brother, Simon Peter,
"We have found the Messiah" (John 1:41b). Chapter 3 records Jesus'
witness to the Pharisee Nicodemus. Finally, chapter 4 presents Jesus'
witness to the woman at the well, which led to her conversion so that
she, too, became a witness for Christ.

Obviously, it was important to John that Christians should be witnesses for Jesus and His gospel. In all likelihood, it was important to

John because it was important to Jesus: in Luke's version of the Great Commission, Jesus placed our witness on equal footing with His death and resurrection: "Thus it is written, that the Christ should suffer and on the third day rise from the dead, and that repentance and forgiveness of sins should be proclaimed in his name" (Luke 24:46–47a). This great statement helps us to see our witness in its proper place. God's saving plan relies on Christ's death, Christ's resurrection, and the witness of Christ's church. In this present age, our witness is the way Jesus is bringing salvation to the world.

The Woman's Witness Proved Her New Birth

As we conclude our study of Jesus' encounter with the woman at the well, we learn a number of lessons about a Christian witness. The first is that *her witness was proof of her new birth.* In the previous chapter, I pointed out that by leaving her water jar, the woman showed that there had been a change in her worldly way of thinking. In the same way, a change in our values and lifestyles is a necessary sign of the new birth. But Christianity involves much more than leaving behind a sinful, worldly life. It also involves living discipleship with Jesus, one vital aspect of which is that we tell others what we have found. This is exactly what happened with this woman. John records that she "went away into town and said to the people, 'Come, see a man who told me all that I ever did. Can this be the Christ?'" (John 4:28b–29).

Hers was a powerful witness, because it presented Jesus through the lens of her own changed heart. It seems that she was an immoral woman who was shunned by her neighbors, so her sinful past surely would have been a sore subject with her. But once she had been born again, instead of being ashamed of what she had done, she blurted out that Jesus knew all about it. This is one of the most important signs that people have truly come to faith in Christ: instead of covering their sin and resenting the subject, true Christians publicly admit their sin—in fact, they delight to do so—in order to show that Jesus is the Savior of sinners. This is how the new birth changes us into witnesses for Christ, and it is because people notice this change that they listen and come. In this way, the new birth both causes and empowers our witness to Christ.

The Samaritan woman's witness had two essential elements that any Christian witness must include: she told people what she knew about the Lord and she invited them to meet Him for themselves. Hers was like Andrew's witness to his brother, Simon Peter: Andrew said, "We have found the Messiah" (John 1:41), and brought Simon to Jesus. If nothing else, all Christians should be able to tell what they have found in Jesus and invite people, saying, "Come and see!" This is how the majority of people come to Christ today: they hear a heart-felt testimony and receive an invitation to a church service or a Bible study, where they encounter Jesus for themselves.

The Woman's Witness Excited Jesus

A second thing we notice about Christian witness in this story is that *the woman's witness was thrilling for Jesus.* His reaction came out in His reply to the disciples when they returned with food. They urged Him, "'Rabbi, eat.' But he said to them, 'I have food to eat that you do not know about.' So the disciples said to one another, 'Has anyone brought him something to eat?' Jesus said to them, 'My food is to do the will of him who sent me and to accomplish his work'" (John 4:31b–34).

Most people have some interest in which they can become so engrossed that their bodily needs are practically forgotten. For some it is classical music; while Bach is played, they hardly even breathe. Others are this way about fishing; while reeling in a great marlin, they are lost in a heart-pounding euphoria that removes all hunger and thirst. Jesus feels this way about the saving of souls. What great news this is for us! Jesus' passion is our salvation!

This portion of the story shows us the importance of our witness to Christ. Jesus must have been watching the Samaritan woman on her way back to Sychar, excited by His knowledge that she was born again.

Surely He asked the Father to fan the spark of her faith and bless her witness. Perhaps Jesus gave thought to His words of greeting to the people she was going to bring. He was completely caught up in the spread of His gospel, so much so that when the disciples offered Him food—and remember that Jesus was weary, thirsty, and most likely hungry when He and His disciples reached Sychar—He replied, "I have food to eat that you do not know about." Jesus was exhilarated by the woman's new birth and her witness, so He had no thought for physical food.

What does this tell us about Jesus' view of our world and its affairs today? Surely it is literally the case that the things that make front-page news are of comparatively little interest to Him. What rulers are decreeing, what polls are showing, what stock prices are doing—much less the sports scores—are affairs of the worldly kingdom but not of Christ's kingdom. During His life, He paid no attention to military, political, or economic affairs. But He wearied Himself down the Samaritan road to save this woman's soul, and her witness to her neighbors was of compelling interest to our Lord. Does this not challenge our own priorities and interests? Even though we have earthly duties, isn't what truly matters in every arena not the things of worldly concern but those things that advance the gospel and glorify God? Isn't it true that what really matters is not how much money you make or how your career is advanced but how you witness for Christ and glorify Him in your life?

A telling chapter in C. S. Lewis' *The Screwtape Letters* makes this very point. This chilling book envisions letters between demons regarding how to ensnare and destroy souls. Lewis was writing during the darkest days of World War II, and in one of the letters the junior demon rejoices because his subject may be drafted into the army and perhaps even killed. But his superior demon points out that the war itself—even his subject's death—matters far less than the spiritual response occasioned by the war. The key, he points out, is to use the war to cultivate hatred or self-boasting pride of reckless folly. He warns that their Enemy (that is, Jesus Christ) often uses terrible things like wars to make people think about eternity, inspire compassion, and spread the message of salvation through His gospel.[1] This is how Christians should think, too, even about important matters like wars. What matters most is not the rising and falling of nations but the harvesting of souls either for heaven or hell. Our most central concern in every situation should be the same as Christ's: the witness we are giving to the gospel of His salvation.

Jesus applied this as a general principle: "My food is to do the will of him who sent me and to accomplish his work" (John 4:34). These two priorities consumed His mind and heart: He was committed to acting in conformity with God's will and to completing the task God had given Him to do. This commitment on Jesus' part sets an agenda for how we, too, can lead fulfilling lives despite hardships or trials—by committing ourselves to godly living and faithful service to God.

The divergence between Jesus' focus and our own explains the unhappiness and lack of fulfillment many of us experience, even as Christians. Do you realize that the more self-centered we are, the more unhappy and unfulfilled we are? Are you trying to feast on an unwholesome diet of worldly amusements, earthly success, or sinful pleasure? You will never be satisfied that way! Too many Christians can recite details of all the sit-coms on television but do not know what to say to lead a sinner to Christ. Many others feed richly on God's Word, but because they do not serve—and especially because they do not witness—they find themselves strangely unfulfilled.

The way to lead a joyful, meaningful life is not to pursue your own pleasure but to do everything to the glory of God. This means leaving behind the clay water jars of sin and worldly ambition. It means delighting to do God's will and to serve His kingdom. Above all else, as Jesus shows us, our chief delight should be playing a role in the salvation of other people. Is there a greater thrill than to lead another person to Christ? I have known many excitements in life, but none surpasses playing the least role in the salvation of a human being through faith in Christ. What Jesus said should be true of us as well: "My food is to do the will of him who sent me and to accomplish his work."

The Woman's Witness Encourages Us

The woman's witness not only revealed that she was born again and excited our Lord, *it encourages us by its success.* The townspeople followed her to Jesus, and "Many Samaritans from that town believed in him because of the woman's testimony. . . . They asked him to stay with them, and he stayed there two days. And many more believed because of his word" (John 4:39–41).

Many Christians do not witness because they fear that no one will respond in faith. If this fear is keeping you from sharing the gospel, take note of the effect of the woman's witness among the people of Sychar. And note also three encouragements for witnessing that Jesus provided in the context of this story.

The first is that His coming brought a time of spiritual harvest to the world. Jesus said, "Do you not say, 'There are yet four months, then comes the harvest'? Look, I tell you, lift up your eyes, and see that the fields are white for harvest" (John 4:35).

Jesus stated a local proverb, which held that there are four months of tending crops before a harvest is reaped. But in spiritual terms, His coming indicated that the time of harvest had arrived. What did He mean by saying "the fields are white"? One answer is that Sychar was part of a region known for its corn. We do not know the exact season in which Jesus passed through this place, but it may have been that He could wave His hand to indicate surrounding fields with ripe corn stalks, symbolic of the harvest of souls made possible by His coming. Another suggestion is made by H. V. Morton, who wrote of his visit to this very place: "As I sat by Jacob's Well a crowd of Arabs came along the road from the direction in which Jesus was looking, and I saw their white garments shining in the sun. Surely Jesus was speaking not of the earthly but of the heavenly harvest, and as He spoke I think it likely that He pointed along the road where the Samaritans in their white robes were assembling to hear his words."[2] In either case, Jesus' point was that what previously seemed impossible was now quite possible by the heavenly power He had brought.

Think how unlikely it was that all the people of a town in Samaria would be converted to faith in a Jewish teacher, much less by the witness of a woman they previously had despised. But the most unlikely people can believe the gospel and be saved today—through the most unlikely witnesses—because Jesus' coming brings a glorious harvest of souls.

John G. Paton brought the gospel to the cannibals in the New Hebrides Islands. People tried to dissuade him from going, arguing that it was impossible to convert savages and that he most likely would be killed and eaten. But Paton was possessed by the same passion that fed the heart of our Lord. He wrote, "I was sustained by the lofty aim which burned all these years bright within my soul, namely to be owned and used by Him for the salvation of perishing men. . . . The wail and claims of the heathen were constantly sounding in my ears. I saw them perishing for lack of the knowledge of the true God and His Son Jesus."[3]

But when Paton arrived in the South Seas, even he was shocked by the depravity of the cannibals. The account of his many miraculous deliverances is amazing and glorious to God. But what is most glorious is the display of the gospel's power through the conversion of an entire island of violent natives. Paton lived among the people, learning their language, translating the Bible, and proclaiming the gospel. He announced God's judgment on their sins and forgiveness through the atoning death of God's Son. One of his biographers noted how his harvest was won: "The Word of God brought conviction of sin and begot faith, and this faith brought forth 'works meet for repentance."[4] In other words, Paton simply gave witness to the gospel, as we are to do, and he found, as Jesus promised, that the fields were "white for harvest," even in the most unlikely of places.

Second, Jesus used the Samaritan woman's success to point out how great is the reward of our witness: "Already the one who reaps is receiving wages and gathering fruit for eternal life, so that sower and reaper may rejoice together" (John 4:36). Not only can we expect success through our witness, but the value is incalculable—the salvation of people from eternal damnation. Leon Morris writes: "The task is not some insignificant one, where it does not matter much whether or not it is done. Jesus is talking about work in a field where the eternal welfare of people is at stake."[5]

Third, Jesus said that we often will reap where others have sown: "For here the saying holds true, 'One sows and another reaps.' I sent you to reap that for which you did not labor. Others have labored, and you have entered into their labor" (John 4:37–38). This was true even with these Samaritans. Jesus and the woman had sown the gospel, but theirs was not the first witness to this region. For instance, John the Baptist had preached nearby (John 3:23). We also know that the Samaritans believed the five books of the Pentateuch, so Moses' long-past labor was bearing fruit among them, too. Now the disciples of Jesus could reap the harvest. Years after Jesus was there, Philip the deacon would come to Samaria and lead many to salvation, perhaps following up with some of the very people who met Jesus through the woman's witness (Acts 8).

If God uses your witness to save someone, realize that you are almost certainly reaping where someone else has sown. This is Christ's blessing to you: He said, "I sent you to reap that for which you did not labor" (John 4:38). Indeed, there could be no salvation without Jesus having sown the seed of His life on the cross. We are able to reap because of the forgiveness He has sown through His own blood.

Even when we do not get to see the results for which we long—when our witness apparently does not lead to faith and salvation—we can rejoice to know that others may come and reap from our witness. We are not responsible for the outcome, but only for our faithful, loving witness. Yet we speak to others about Jesus with a great hope, knowing that He is mighty to save through the combined witness of His many people.

Jesus' statement in John 4:37 makes clear that sometimes we will sow but not reap, whereas other times we will reap because others sowed. Before Paton's great success among the South Sea cannibals, he spent several years on the island of Tanna with much labor and sacrifice—including the death of his wife and son—only to be driven away. Despite Paton's great faith, his first, painful venture was an apparent failure. But he kept at it, and on another island, Aniwa, God gave him such success that the whole island became a beacon of Christian godliness. So what about Tanna? Some time after Paton departed from Aniwa, the believers there sent a mission to Tanna, and those witnesses enjoyed a great harvest of conversions on the ground once sown with Paton's labor and tears. That glorious harvest—like all successful outreach—should encourage our own witness.

The Woman's Witness Revealed Jesus as Savior of the World

I want to conclude with the statement that came from the lips of these Samaritan converts: "They said to the woman, 'It is no longer because of what you said that we believe, for we have heard for ourselves, and we know that this is indeed the Savior of the world'" (John 4:42). Her witness did not have to save them; indeed, it could not do so. She merely led them to Jesus and He did the rest. Their salvation reveals the great fact that motivates our evangelistic witness: Jesus is the Savior of the world.

Do you realize this? Do you realize it when you think about other people you know? There is no savior for their souls in all this world other than Jesus Christ. Yes, a doctor may save them from disease. An employer may save them from poverty. But what about death? What about God's judgment on sin? What about the eternity that awaits beyond the grave? Jesus is the only One who can save us from sin, death, and God's just wrath. What good will you have done others if you befriended them or spent time with them in some worthy cause, yet did not tell them about the world's only Savior, apart from whom they must perish forever? What kind of love is this—to know Jesus as the Savior of the world, yet fail to tell people who do not know Him? Surely, if the spark of new life is burning in our souls and we have the slightest shred of Christ's love for people, we will at least do what this Samaritan woman did. Surely we can risk a little embarrassment or inconvenience to tell people, "I have found the Savior: Come and see!"

If you have never understood this and have never trusted Christ for yourself, let me have the privilege of urging you to do so now. When the Samaritans called Jesus "the Savior of the world," they did not mean that everyone in the world will be saved. The Gospel of John is very clear that many will perish in sin. John reports Jesus' own sobering words: "Whoever believes in [me] is not condemned, but whoever does not believe is condemned already, because he has not believed in the name of the only Son of God" (John 3:18). What the Samaritans meant is that Jesus is such a Savior that even the most unlikely people—and that is what the Samaritans were in that day—can be saved simply by coming to Him in faith. There are no sins so dark that they cannot be washed clean by His atoning blood. There is no rebel so outcast before God that he will not be received through God's own Son. It is Jesus' passion—the food that consumes His heart—to do God's work of salvation for everyone in the world who will come. Let us not fail to receive the Savior of the world as our own Savior, that we might then enter into His harvest of eternal life. And let us not fail to tell the world.

NOTES

[1] C. S. Lewis, *The Screwtape Letters* (Westwood, N.J.: Barbour Books, 1990), ch. 5.

[2] Cited from William Barclay, *The Gospel of John*, 2 vols. (Philadelphia, Pa.: Westminster, 1975), 1:167–168.

[3] John D. Legg, "John G. Paton: Missionary of the Cross," in *Five Pioneering Missionaries* (Edinburgh, Scotland, and Carlisle, Pa.: Banner of Truth Trust, 1965), 309.

[4] Ibid., 325.

[5] Leon Morris, *Reflections on the Gospel of John* (Peabody, Mass.: Hendrickson Publishers, 1986), 151.

Questions for discussion and reflection:

1. Is it possible for someone who is born again *not* to witness the gospel? Why is a desire to tell others about Jesus such an important proof of new life in Christ?

2. The Samaritan woman boldly used her past failures as a vehicle for sharing what Jesus had done for her. Are there ways in which you have done this or can do it? What are some potential pitfalls? What are some opportunities?

3. What does it mean to realize that Jesus is watching our witness, just as He watched the Samaritan woman returning to her village? What do you think Jesus is doing as you witness in His name?

4. What features of the Samaritan woman's example encourage you to be bolder in your witness? Do you think you could lead someone to salvation through faith in Jesus? What would enable you to do so?

5. Reflect on the proverbial sayings Jesus spoke regarding evangelism. How do they encourage you to persevere in your witness to Christ? How do Jesus' words help you endure hardship for the sake of His gospel?

6. The Samaritan converts glorified Jesus as "the Savior of the world." Spend some time in prayer thanking Jesus for what He has done for you and for others. Reflect on the major lessons you have gained from your study of this book and how you expect to be bolder and more effective as an evangelist.

THE SOVEREIGNTY OF GOD IN EVANGELISM

Therefore, having this ministry by the mercy of God, we do not lose heart. But we have renounced disgraceful, under-handed ways. We refuse to practice cunning or to tamper with God's word, but by the open statement of the truth we would commend ourselves to everyone's conscience in the sight of God.   *—2 Corinthians 4:1–2*

Whenever Reformed Christians begin to discuss evangelism, the topic of God's sovereignty is bound to come up.

Because the Bible teaches that God has predestined all those who enter into eternal life, some argue that it is wrong or point-less to labor in evangelism. Having written this book to stress biblical evangelism, this is obviously not my view. And in light of our studies in John's Gospel, it is equally obvious—and far more important—that this was not Jesus' view. The book of Acts reveals the same when it comes to the apostles.

Others within the Reformed community joyfully believe in the sov-ereignty of God in salvation, but this belief seems to exert little or no influence on their approach to evangelism. The way in which they carry out this duty suggests that they are practicing Arminians. This does not seem right either.

Anticipating questions about how our witness relates to divine sovereignty, I thought it would be helpful to provide an appendix commenting on this important matter. For help, I want to turn to the classic treatment of this subject, which was given by J. I. Packer in his book *Evangelism and the Sovereignty of God.*[1] The material in this appendix does not all come from Packer's fine treatment of the subject, but I would recommend that everyone interested in this topic—indeed, every Christian—read his important book.

Packer defines evangelism as "just preaching the gospel, the evangel. It is a work of communication in which Christians make themselves mouth-pieces for God's message of mercy to sinners."[2] Packer argues that our goal in evangelism is not to convert sinners, since power for this lies beyond our ability, but to present the biblical message about Jesus faithfully. This message consists of "the gospel of Christ, and Him crucified; the message of man's sin and God's grace, of human guilt and divine forgiveness, of new birth and new life through the gift of the Holy Spirit."[3]

Taking this definition of evangelism as a starting point, I will address the topic in three points: 1) Does God's sovereignty argue against evangelism? 2) Does God's sovereignty actually encourage evangelism? and 3) How should our belief in God's sovereignty reform our approach to evangelism?

Does God's Sovereignty Argue against Evangelism?

A study of the New Testament clearly shows that Christians are called to the task of evangelism, if for no other reason than the examples of both Jesus and the apostles. This calling in itself indicates that evangelism and the sovereignty of God are not in conflict, but I would note five other reasons why there is no opposition.

The first is that *divine sovereignty does not rule out human will and responsibility*. The problem, as some see it, is this: if salvation is based on a decision God made before time, then what people do today seems not to matter. The Bible indeed teaches that God "predestined us for adoption through Jesus Christ, according to the purpose of his will" (Eph. 1:5). But the conclusion that predestination eliminates the need for evangelism errs by considering only part of the Bible's teaching. A similar error is made in the other direction by those who deny predestination because of Bible passages in which people are commanded to choose in favor of God. It is true that Joshua told Israel, "Choose this day whom you will serve. . . . But as for me and my house, we will serve the LORD" (Josh. 24:15). This statement, however, does not overrule Jesus' statement to the disciples: "You did not choose me, but I chose you" (John 15:16a). Neither does the Bible's teaching of divine election overrule the fact that the Bible does require us to exercise faith in Christ.

The reality is that the Bible teaches both divine predestination and full human responsibility. Our theology must be able to incorporate both Ephesians 1:5 and Joshua 24:15; that is, both the many passages that speak of God's utter sovereignty in salvation and those that declare man's utter responsibility before God. The best way to begin to deal with this issue is to realize that the Bible vigorously teaches both truths.

We will never be able to penetrate fully the mystery of how divine predestination and human responsibility go together, just as we will never fully understand how Jesus can be both fully God and fully man. But some biblical reflection will help. Take Judas Iscariot. His betrayal of our Lord was prophesied in the Psalms (Ps. 41:9) and also by Jesus (Mark 14:18–20). The Old Testament even foretold how many pieces of silver Judas would be paid (Zech. 11:12–13). But is he thereby excused for betraying our Lord? Not at all; Judas is plainly condemned as responsible for his wicked deeds. Indeed, Jesus ascribed full responsibility to Judas for his actions. For instance, when Jesus excluded Judas from the Last Supper, He remarked to him, "What you are going to do, do quickly" (John 13:27). It really was Judas who betrayed Jesus, even though it had been prophesied long beforehand and happened, as Peter remarked, "according to the definite plan and foreknowledge of God" (Acts 2:23).

The most powerful biblical example is Jesus Christ Himself. Here is One whose life was not merely predestined, but prerecorded in many of its details. Yet who will call God's Son a puppet, without will and responsibility? Think about Jesus' death. Peter directly ascribed Christ's death to God's election (see again Acts 2:23). But he concluded that verse by assigning blame to the Jews who despised Him: "You, with the help of wicked men, put him to death by nailing him to the cross" (NIV). Divine sovereignty and human responsibility stand side by side in Scripture. We do not have to reconcile them, but we must accept that God asserts them both.

Understanding this, we see why God's complete sovereignty does not eliminate the need for us to appeal to the will of men in evangelism. People really do exercise choice, and the choice they make regarding Jesus Christ has eternal implications. Therefore, Christians should fervently communicate the gospel to others.

There is a second reason why divine sovereignty does not stand against evangelism—*because God ordains not merely the ends but also the means.* He predestines some to be saved and commands us to preach the gospel to that end. If we do not preach and teach the gospel, then none will be saved. But God has ordained that some will be redeemed; He has chosen His people to be saved. So He also has ordained that we should preach and share the gospel, and therefore we will, exercising our human responsibility in accordance with His sovereign purpose. God commands all who are His to engage in evangelism; it is part of our obedience to Him. Packer explains: "We are not all called to be preachers; we are not all given equal opportunities or comparable abilities for personal dealing with men and women who need Christ. But we all have some evangelistic responsibility which we cannot shirk without failing in love both to our God and to our neighbor."[4]

As a divinely ordained means to an end, evangelism is analogous to prayer. Sam Storms offers an example of how prayer serves as a means

God has provided to accomplish the ends He has ordained. Suppose God has decided that a man named Gary will be saved through faith in Christ on August 8. Suppose, also, that unbeknownst to me, God wills to bring him to faith in response to my prayer for Gary on August 7. Storms asks:

> Does this mean that God's will for Gary's salvation on the eighth might fail should I forget or refuse to pray on the seventh? No. We must remember that God has decreed or willed my praying on the seventh for Gary's salvation, which he intends to effect on the eighth. God does not will the end, that is, Gary's salvation on the eighth, apart from the means, that is, my prayer on the seventh. . . . From a human perspective, it may rightly be said that God's will for Gary is dependent upon me and my prayers, as long as it is understood that God, by an infallible decree, has secured and guaranteed my prayers as an instrument with no less certainty than he has secured and guaranteed Gary's faith as an end.[5]

Why, some then will ask, should we bother praying and evangelizing, if it is all decreed by God? The answer, of course, is that we do not know what God has ordained until it happens. Having Gary's salvation on my heart, what else should I do but pray and use every opportunity to lead him to faith and salvation, trusting that God will bless these means as He is so often glad to do?

A third reason why evangelism is compatible with God's sovereignty is that *evangelism is one of the best ways to glorify God.* Packer writes: "We glorify God by evangelizing . . . because in evangelism we tell the world what great things God has done for the salvation of sinners. God is glorified when His mighty works of grace are made known. . . . For a Christian to talk to the unconverted about the Lord Jesus Christ and His saving power is in itself honouring and glorifying to God."[6]

Moreover, *evangelism is one of the best ways to fulfill God's command that we love our neighbors.* We are commanded to desire good for others, and what greater good could there be than to seek the salvation of our fellow men and women? With this in mind, every Christian should ask:

"Should I not be regularly in prayer for the conversion of at least one person I know? Should I not be asking God for opportunities to witness the gospel and also preparing myself as best I can to make good use of the opportunities that God provides?"

Our knowledge that not all are elect does not argue against evangelism. The reality is that we simply do not know who is and who is not elect until someone believes in Christ. Many people who do not presently believe are in fact elect; every Christian was once in this position. God calls us to love not just the elect but to love our neighbors as ourselves, and the highest form of love is that which tells sinners about the Savior.

Fifth, as Packer notes, *the sovereignty of God does not invalidate anything that the Bible shows us about our calling to evangelism.* While God is sovereign, it is still necessary that men and women come to faith in Christ, and, as Paul wrote, "How are they to believe in him of whom they have never heard?" (Rom. 10:14b). We simply *must* tell people about Jesus. Packer writes: "If you knew that a man was asleep in a blazing building, you would think it a matter of urgency to try and get to him, and wake him up, and bring him out. The world is full of people who are unaware that they stand under the wrath of God: is it not similarly a matter of urgency that we should go to them, and try to arouse them, and show them the way of escape?"[7]

It is important that we realize that God's sovereignty does not affect the genuineness of the gospel invitation. Packer writes, "The fact remains that God in the gospel really does offer Christ and promise justification and life to 'whosoever will'."[8] This was made explicit by the apostle when he wrote, "Everyone who calls on the name of the Lord will be saved" (Rom. 10:13). If this is not a genuine statement of the gospel's call to everyone—elect and non-elect—then Paul's sincerity is called into question. The same can be said of the many statements with which Jesus offered the crowds His salvation. "Come to me, all who labor and are heavy laden," Jesus cried, "and I will give you rest" (Matt. 11:28). That is a true and genuine offer of salvation. Likewise, Jesus called out, "If anyone thirsts, let him come to me and drink" (John 7:37b). Surely this example of our Lord, making a genuine offer to all the world, should set the standard for our own willingness to share the gospel with one and all.

The great Puritan theologian John Owen wrote: "Consider the infinite condescension and love of Christ, in his invitations and calls of you to come unto him for life, deliverance, mercy, grace, peace and eternal salvation."[9] Christ, he argued, still calls out with His love in the preaching of these invitations: "In the declaration and preaching of them, Jesus Christ yet stands before sinners, calling, inviting, encouraging them to come unto him."[10] Therefore, Christians should point out to everyone the opportunity for salvation that God provides. The responsibility for unbelief lies with man, not with God.

In the same manner, God's sovereignty does not mitigate the sinner's responsibility to believe on Christ. Here, Packer's words cannot be excelled:

> The fact remains that a man who rejects Christ thereby becomes the cause of his own condemnation. . . . The unbeliever was really offered life in the gospel, and could have had it if he would; he, and no one but he, is responsible for the fact that he rejected it. . . . The Bible never says that sinners miss heaven because they are not elect, but because they "neglect the great salvation", and because they will not repent and believe.[11]

Does God's Sovereignty Actually Encourage Evangelism?

Not only does our awareness of God's sovereignty not invalidate our calling to evangelism, but in reality, it actually encourages our witness. Four reasons for this come to mind: the truth of divine sovereignty encourages us to be *dependent* on God in evangelism and *bold, patient,* and *confident* in spreading the gospel.

First, understanding God's sovereignty makes us *dependent* on Him because we see that it is only because of sovereign grace that the conversion of spiritually dead sinners is even possible. The Calvinist knows that unbelievers are not merely sick; they are "dead in . . . trespasses and sins" (Eph. 2:1). We know that people are dead when they no longer respond to stimuli. We talk to them and they do not answer. We touch them and they do not move. This is the way people who are spiritually dead relate to God and His Word. When the Bible is taught, they have no comprehension; when the gospel offer is made, they make no response.

This presents a most depressing situation for an evangelist. Given man's utter depravity, an evangelist cannot hope to lead anyone to faith in Christ by his own power. Paul states, "The natural person does not accept the things of the Spirit of God, for they are folly to him, and he is not able to understand them because they are spiritually discerned" (1 Cor. 2:14). Note that Paul says not only that the natural person "does not" accept the gospel but that he "is not able to." Elsewhere, the apostle says, "The mind that is set on the flesh is hostile to God, for it does not submit to God's law; indeed, it cannot" (Rom. 8:7). Packer therefore writes: "Our approach to evangelism is not realistic till we have faced this shattering fact, and let it make its proper impact on us. . . . Regarded as a human enterprise, evangelism is a hopeless task."[12]

This being the case, our only hope for leading others to salvation comes not from man—neither from the unbeliever nor the Christian witness—but from almighty God. No amount of emotional manipulation or moral persuasion can lead the totally depraved sinner to exercise a nature he or she simply does not possess. But God has invincible power to change the sinner's nature. This was the great promise given through Ezekiel, the promise realized by every believer and relied upon by every evangelist: "I will give you a new heart, and a new spirit I will put within you. And I will remove the heart of stone from your flesh and give you a heart of flesh" (Ezek. 36:26).

Therefore, evangelism is made possible only by the sovereignty of God. We preach Christ knowing that God has predestined many to salvation, that Christ died to "save his people from their sins" (Matt. 1:21b), and that the Holy Spirit will apply the gospel as it is preached and witnessed, in the time of His own choosing, to bring spiritually dead unbelievers to resurrection life. Paul explains: "God, being rich in mercy, because of the great love with which he loved us, even when we were dead in our trespasses, made us alive together with Christ" (Eph. 2:4–5a). This life comes through the gospel by the power of the sovereign grace of God.

Second, it is God's sovereign grace that makes us *bold* in evangelism. This is a matter with which most of us struggle. Can *I* really be used to lead someone to eternal life? Will *my* witness make any difference? When we realize that salvation depends not on human willingness or persuasiveness but "on God, who has mercy" (Rom. 9:16b), then our attitude changes entirely. Indeed, why should God not glorify Himself by using our weakness to display His mighty strength?

I think of this every time I enter a pulpit to preach. I am crushingly aware of my own inability to drive home the gospel to hardened hearts. But then I think: "Why shouldn't God use this sermon to give life to the dead?" This was God's message to Ezekiel, when the prophet stood before the valley of dry bones. "Can these bones live?" God asked him. "O Lord GOD, you know," the prophet wisely answered. "Prophesy over these bones," God commanded him, "and say to them, O dry bones, hear the word of the LORD" (Ezek. 37:3–4). As he preached, Ezekiel witnessed bones and sinews coming together to form bodies, and life from God being breathed into them so that "they lived and stood on their feet, an exceedingly great army" (Ezek. 37:10).

This is the bold assurance our generation needs to have in the power of God through the gospel. In my view, the main reason so much worldliness has flooded into our churches—our obsession with entertainment, our reliance on psychology, and our descent into crass marketing—is our lack of trust in God's power through His Word. We hear the objection all the time: "Surely you don't think we can simply preach the Bible?" But those who know the power of the sovereign God are bold to preach Christ alone, witnessing the gospel of God's grace in reliance on sovereign power from on high. For, God says, "So shall my word be that goes out from my mouth; it shall not return to me empty, but it shall accomplish that which I purpose, and shall succeed in the thing for which I sent it" (Isa. 55:11).

Third, our knowledge of God's sovereignty makes us *patient* in evangelism. Too many Christians either pervert or misrepresent the gospel by their methods precisely because they feel the burden of manufacturing success. But those who rely on God's power are satisfied simply to present the saving truths about Jesus, to pray, and then to wait. We encourage others to read the Bible for themselves. We patiently respond to questions. We refuse to be downcast when our witness does not immediately result in conversion, and neither do we lose interest in people whose conversion entails a longer, more difficult process.

An experience in a church I formerly served underscores this need for patience. A couple began attending our evening service. They had long attended a liberal church that taught nothing of the gospel. But one day the husband announced to his wife that such religion was leaving him empty. She asked what he intended to do, and he informed her that he had been listening to Christian radio. He had heard preaching from our church and decided to attend. Being a devoted wife, she agreed to come with him.

It was not long before the man came to a settled faith in Jesus, but his wife was different. She was often offended by the sermons, especially those that spoke of God's wrath against sin and of Jesus as the world's only Savior. She had many humanistic objections and she thought the preaching intolerant. But being a thoughtful woman, she began corresponding with the preacher through occasional notes. This correspondence lasted for more than a year, while her husband grew in his faith and exercised patient love in his witness to his wife.

I well remember the day that minister came to our staff meeting, beaming with the news that had come with the woman's latest note. She had simply written, "Dear Pastor, the scales have fallen off my eyes." How many prayers were thus answered! How long and patient had been the witness that resulted in this conversion, producing an intelligent, vibrant, and caring believer in Jesus Christ. By God's sovereign grace, it was precisely because no one tried to force an immediate decision from her—one that would violate the sincere, if sinful, objections of her mind—that she finally believed and knew her Savior.

If we take all these encouragements together—that only God's sovereign grace makes conversion possible and that our dependence on God's grace makes us bold and patient in evangelism—we see that the sovereignty of God alone gives us proper grounds to be *confident* in our witness of the gospel. James Montgomery Boice concludes:

> It is only election that gives us any hope of success as we evangelize. If God cannot call people to faith effectively, how can we? We cannot persuade them. But if God is working, then he can work in us even if we are inept witnesses. We do not know who God's elect are, but we can find out who some of them are by telling them about Jesus. . . . We can speak to them boldly because we know that God has promised to bless his Word.[13]

How Should Our Belief in God's Sovereignty Reform Our Approach to Evangelism?

The last topic to consider is one of vital concern to the church today, namely, divine sovereignty and the reform of evangelism. Let me suggest five ways in which our belief in divine sovereignty ought to shape our approach to evangelism.

First, because of God's sovereignty, *our evangelism should be biblical,* both in its message and method. If we witness the gospel because of our obedience to God's Word, certainly this argues that our witness should conform to the teachings of the Bible.

This was Paul's emphasis in his great statement of the principles that informed his own gospel ministry, found in 2 Corinthians 4:1–6. Paul explains that the guiding principle of his ministry was the sovereign mercy of God: "Therefore, having this ministry by the mercy of God, we do not lose heart" (2 Cor. 4:1). What kept Paul going was his realization of God's mercy, both to him and toward all the world. The result was that he disowned all manipulation and tampering in his presentation of the gospel: "But we have renounced disgraceful, underhanded ways. We refuse to practice cunning or to tamper with God's word" (4:2a). So what did Paul do? "By the open statement of the truth we would commend ourselves to everyone's conscience in the sight of God" (4:2b). Paul simply taught the message about Jesus, appealing in this way to the consciences of men and women.

We can well imagine Paul hearing the very objection leveled against this approach today: "But it doesn't always work!" He had a reply to this, namely, that the reason why the gospel does not always produce salvation is not the gospel's failure but the reality of spiritual bondage in our world. He explains: "Even if our gospel is veiled, it is veiled only to those who are perishing. In their case the god of this world has blinded the minds of the unbelievers, to keep them from seeing the light of the gospel of the glory of Christ, who is the image of God" (4:3–4). In other words, resistance to the gospel should not surprise us in a dying world in bondage to the Devil.

But the answer to this problem, Paul continues, lies not in abandoning God's way of evangelism. The answer is to rely on God's power to overcome darkness with the light of His gospel. Paul states this in glorious terms: "For God, who said, 'Let light shine out of darkness,' has shone in our hearts to give the light of the knowledge of the glory of God in the face of Jesus Christ" (4:6). In effect, Paul says: "What a difference it would make if the almighty power of God accompanied the witness of His gospel, so that the very power that first created the universe was now exerted in revealing the glory of Christ in the gospel! And this is exactly what happens when Christ is preached and God sovereignly blesses His Word with the light of Christ!" Salvation is a gift, and it comes through faith in the gospel as it is communicated to sinners.

It is with this in mind that Paul states his key conviction, his own guiding light for evangelism: "For what we proclaim is not ourselves, but Jesus Christ as Lord, with ourselves as your servants for Jesus' sake"

(4:5). What did Paul rely on to lead others to salvation? He preached Christ as Lord, that is, he preached Christ in the fullness of His saving work. He did not preach himself, except as a servant of this gospel, but instead, as he writes elsewhere, "We preach Christ crucified" (1 Cor. 1:23a). Paul did not market the byproducts of Christian faith—that is, he did not preach family values, good relationships, and success at work, much less instant financial prosperity! Instead, he preached the saving work of Jesus on the cross to reconcile sinners to a holy God. "I believed, and so I spoke," Paul explains (2 Cor. 4:13). This commitment characterized not only Paul's ministry but the evangelistic labors of all the apostles. As Peter explained to the Christians under his charge: "You have been born again, not of perishable seed but of imperishable, through the living and abiding word of God" (1 Peter 1:23). Likewise, our faith in the Bible should lead us to biblical evangelism.

Let me apply this principle practically. Relying on God's sovereign power, we should be committed to God's ways as taught in the Bible. This means that our evangelism should consist of explaining as clearly and lovingly as we can the facts concerning Jesus as taught in the Bible. Here, Packer's conclusion is beyond improvement:

> The test for any proposed strategy, or technique, or style, of evangelistic action must be this: will it in fact serve the word? Is it calculated to be a means of explaining the gospel truly and fully and applying it deeply and exactly? To the extent to which it is so calculated, it is lawful and right; to the extent to which it tends to overlay and obscure the realities of the message, and to blunt the edge of their application, it is ungodly and wrong. . . . Is this way of presenting Christ calculated to promote, or impede, the work of the word in men's minds?[14]

Another practical implication of our commitment to biblical evange-lism is a refusal to employ unbiblical methods, and especially deceitful manipulation. Yet the operative assumption of modern revivalism is that we must employ persuasive techniques despite their lack of biblical warrant.

The prime example is the altar call. Evangelists observe that faith in Christ is accompanied by a public testimony. Therefore, they wrongly (and, I believe, harmfully) assume that if they can induce the public testimony, they may assume the inward reality of faith. To this end, long appeals are made, including all manner of attempts to induce the physical act of "walking the sawdust trail." The preacher will call for a time of prayer and ask people to raise their hands if they are praying for salvation. In many cases—and some revivalists are honest enough to admit it—already converted volunteers are led down the aisle or placed to raise their hands, all in order to present a powerful spectacle of conversions and thus induce unbelievers to join in the experience. Such techniques and others like them involve dishonest manipulation, the very thing Paul forswore. Not only do they lack any biblical warrant—a perusal of the Gospels and the book of Acts will show nothing of this sort in the ministries of Jesus and the apostles—they are actually harmful in inducing unconverted sinners to suppose that their experience is indicative of genuine, saving faith. Does this mean that no one has truly been saved by these means? Not at all, for as Paul noted, God is merciful. But such unbiblical techniques have done much harm in recent generations and may have led more people away from Christ than they brought to Him.

A second area of needed reform in evangelism is a renewed commitment to prayer. Simply put, because of God's sovereignty, *our evangelism should be prayerful.* James' precept, "You do not have, because you do not ask" (James 4:2b), is felt keenly in our failure to lead more people to Christ. But if we truly realize that God is sovereign in the granting of salvation, and if we remember that the sovereign God is eager to graciously answer our prayers, we will fervently petition him in the matter of evangelism.

Here again, Paul presents a fine example. Consider Ephesians 1, often referred to by those who teach predestination. This chapter includes Paul's great hymn of praise to the saving grace of our triune

God. He praises God the Father for His electing grace, God the Son for His atoning grace, and God the Spirit for His illuminating grace. But what does Paul do immediately upon the conclusion of this most exalted section of teaching? Does he pat himself on the back for the superiority of his doctrine? Does he malign lesser Christians who have yet to attain to such excellence? Not at all. Paul immediately turns to God in prayer. This is because an awareness of God's sovereign grace should always lead to prayer, both in praise and in petition for the success of the gospel.

In fact, it is clear that having delivered his great teaching on God's sovereign grace, Paul was keenly aware of his need to pray. He obviously did not think it sufficient simply to set forth his teaching unless he combined it with fervent prayer to God for His blessing. Speaking of ministers, Arthur W. Pink explains:

> The preacher's obligations are not fully discharged when he leaves the pulpit, for he needs to water the seed he has sown. . . . Paul mingled supplications with his instructions. . . . It is our [preachers'] privilege and duty to retire to the secret place after we leave the pulpit and beg God to write His Word on the hearts of those who have listened to us, to prevent the enemy from snatching away the seed, to so bless our efforts that they may bear fruit to God's eternal praise.[15]

Likewise, all evangelists have a need to pray for God's blessing on their witness of the gospel.

This need highlights a potential danger that arises from our high view of Scripture. We believe and proclaim the sufficiency of Scripture for life and godliness, for the knowledge of God and salvation. Yet that does not make the blessing of Scripture automatic. The doctrine of Scripture's sufficiency does not in any way lessen the need for prayer. God's Word is the singular instrument He has given for building up His church, but it only "works" as God causes it to work. Salvation requires not merely the preaching of God's Word or the witness of the gospel, but also the ministry of the Holy Spirit to regenerate the sinful heart and enlighten the darkened mind, and for this we are to pray.

Donald Grey Barnhouse was one who set an example of combining gospel preaching with humble prayer. He often could be found in the sanctuary on Saturdays, kneeling beside each pew, thinking about the people who often sat there, and asking God to bless them with the following day's sermon. Surely we should likewise pray for those we are hoping to speak to about the gospel of Christ. And having shared the gospel, we must water God's Word with prayers for His blessing in bestowing new life and the gift of faith.

This is precisely what we find at the end of Ephesians 1, where the apostle put down his pen after the elevated teaching of the chapter and petitioned God to enlighten his readers' hearts that they might come to know Him better (Eph. 1:15–21). If that kind of prayer was necessary to Paul, surely it is necessary for us.

Third, because God is sovereign, *our evangelism should be personal.* We see this in the great statement at the beginning of John 4, the chapter that tells of Jesus' personal witness to the Samaritan woman at the well. John says that Jesus "had to pass through Samaria" (John 4:4). Jesus went out of His way to bring the gospel to this one woman, and through her to a whole village. Likewise, knowing that the sovereign God is pleased to call many to salvation, our witness should be courteous and should be infused with the same love for people that moved God to send His Son into the world.

Fourth, because God is sovereign, *our evangelism should be zealous and creative.* We see the labor Jesus expended, since He knew that God's sovereign reign is extended in the gathering of precious souls. Jesus was also creative, taking any topic and using it to draw connections to the gospel. With the proud Pharisee, Nicodemus, Jesus spoke of his need to be born again. To the thirsty Samaritan woman, Jesus offered "living water" (John 4:10b). When a hungry crowd needed to be fed, Jesus performed His miracle with the fishes and loaves, then went on to proclaim Himself "the bread of life" (John 6:35a). The examples from Jesus' ministry are legion; just look through the Gospels and you will see them. Likewise, Christians can and should employ the arts, acts of mercy, military and business experiences, sports programs, and service ministries of all kinds as creative vehicles for presenting the saving truth of Jesus. Such approaches should never take the place of gospel truth and should not marginalize serious Bible teaching, but they can be employed in natural and creative ways to introduce opportunities to connect people to Jesus.

Last, because God is sovereign, *we should never lose heart in evangelism.* I often think of Paul, sent by Jesus to the sordid city of Corinth. I get the impression that Paul didn't think much of the prospects there, and there were clearly some strong obstacles to the success of his ministry in that city. So Jesus appeared to Paul in a vision, saying: "Do not be afraid, but go on speaking and do not be silent, for I am with you, and no one will attack you to harm you, for I have many in this city who are my people" (Acts 18:9b–10). God has many people in the world, and they need to be called through the witness of His gospel. This thought should keep us going even in the face of opposition or spiritual barrenness.

Given his earlier experience, I think it is especially meaningful that it was to the Corinthians that Paul later wrote, "Therefore, having this ministry by the mercy of God, we do not lose heart" (2 Cor. 4:1). Since the success of our witness does not rely on human factors of any kind, but on God's sovereign mercy, let us persevere in the place to which God has called us and in the gospel ministry He has given us. More than that, let our witness be filled with joy, knowing that God's glory is exhibited through the most unlikely displays of His sovereign grace. As Paul exhorted his Corinthian brothers and sisters, let us also be encouraged in the gospel work of our gracious, sovereign God: "Therefore, my beloved brothers, be steadfast, immovable, always abounding in the work of the Lord, knowing that in the Lord your labor is not in vain" (1 Cor. 15:58).

NOTES

1. J. I. Packer, *Evangelism and the Sovereignty of God* (Downers Grove, Ill.: InterVarsity Press, 1991).

2. Ibid., 41.

3. Ibid., 57.

4. Ibid., 78.

5. C. Samuel Storms, "Prayer and Evangelism under God's Sovereignty," in *Still Sovereign: Contemporary Perspectives on Election, Foreknowledge, and Grace,* ed. Thomas R. Schreiner and Bruce A. Ware (Grand Rapids, Mich.: Baker Books, 1995), 316.

6. Packer, *Evangelism and the Sovereignty of God,* 75.

7. Ibid., 98–99.

8. Ibid., 100.

9. John Owen, *Works,* 16 vols. (Edinburgh, Scotland, and Carlisle, Pa.: Banner of Truth Trust, 1991), 1:422.

10. Ibid.

11. Packer, *Evangelism and the Sovereignty of God,* 105. This section of material regarding how God's sovereignty does not invalidate the Bible's call to evangelism roughly follows Packer's writing on pp. 96–105.

12. Ibid., 109.

13. James Montgomery Boice, *Amazing Grace* (Wheaton, Ill.: Tyndale House, 1993), 56.

14. Packer, *Evangelism and the Sovereignty of God,* 86–87.

15. Arthur W. Pink, *The Ability of God: The Prayers of the Apostle Paul* (Chicago, Ill.: Moody Press, 2000), 15.

Index of Scripture

Index of Subjects and Names

About the Author

Richard D. Phillips is senior minister of Second Presbyterian Church in Greenville, S.C., having served previously as pastor of First Presbyterian Church in Coral Springs/Margate, Florida, and as minister of preaching at Tenth Presbyterian Church in Philadelphia. He serves on the council of the Alliance of Confessing Evangelicals and as chairman of the Philadelphia Conference on Reformed Theology.

He earned his bachelor's degree at the University of Michigan, a master of business administration degree at the University of Pennsylvania's Wharton School of Business, and a master of divinity degree at Westminster Theological Seminary. Prior to entering the ministry, he commanded tank units as an officer in the U.S. Army and later served as an assistant professor of leadership at the U.S. Military Academy at West Point.

Rev. Phillips is the author of numerous books, including his most recent, *Hebrews* (part of the Reformed Expository Commentary series) and *Holding Hands, Holding Hearts: Recovering a Biblical View of Christian Dating*, co-written with his wife, Sharon.

The Phillipses live in Greenville, S.C., with their five children, Hannah, Matthew, Jonathan, Helen, and Lydia.